Dear Nita,

Thank you for being my minister, teacher, mentor and friend during this time in my life and for always! I couldn't have gotten through this time with the grace and joy I had without all I learned from you. You have sent so many ripples of love, kindness, compassion and strength out into the world. Words cannot express my gratitude.

With love, Susan

A JOYFUL SEASON *of* SORROW

Susan J. Smith

A Joyful Season of Sorrow
by Susan J. Smith

Published by Susan J. Smith

Copyright © 2024 Susan J. Smith

All rights reserved. No portion of this book may be reproduced in any form without permission from the publisher, except as permitted by U.S. copyright law. For permissions contact: ssmith3858@gmail.com

ISBN: 979-8-35097-631-1 (paperback)
ISBN: 979-8-35097-632-8 (ebook)

DEDICATION

To my mom, Jerry, who taught me to never stop learning and developing; to my dad, Fred, who taught me to live life with unbounded joy and enthusiasm; to my sister, Sandy, who taught me how to be brave and live big; and to my sister, Karen, who taught me about generosity. To all of them for loving me and for the timeless love we share.

INTRODUCTION

A Joyful Season of Sorrow is a story of how myself, my sister Sandy and my Mom Jerry found joy amidst an exceedingly difficult holiday season in 2011. That year on Thanksgiving Day, I became the full-time caretaker for both Mom and Sandy as they became seriously and mysteriously ill at the same time. On the evening and early morning of December 17/18th they both entered the hospital for treatment and soon after they were both diagnosed with terminal illnesses within days of each other. By the end of New Year's Day, they both had died. They were the last two remaining members of my close-knit immediate family. It was indeed a sorrowful time. For me it was difficult to see my family members be in such pain and not know what was wrong or be able to find immediate help for them. Eventually, it was very painful to realize that they would be leaving me so soon. It was also difficult to know whether or not I was doing all I could to help ease them through the incredible pain and suffering they were enduring.

I also looked back on my memories of this time and remember the joy we shared. Fortunately, for me, my New Thought (Unity) spiritual practices and belief system provided both a solid foundation, and a source of practical tools to use so I could show up, I think, as fully present and helpful as possible to them. Mom and Sandy were both incredibly strong, courageous, and patient through this difficult time. I kept some notes and jotted down a few things I knew I wanted to remember about what happened to us during this time. Since I knew they would no longer be able to remember this time alongside me it was especially important that I memorialize the love, peace, grace, and joy that we shared amidst circumstances I don't think any of us could have imagined finding ourselves in. This is a personal memoir of that time, and at the end I provide an analysis of how I applied the spiritual principles that allowed me to thrive amidst what was happening to our family. This is the story of the 3 of us told through my personal lens as I am the one of us that survived to the tell story. I'm sorry I don't have more insight to share about what they were going through at the time, and my intention here is to share what they were going through as best as I possibly can.

Mostly this is a spiritual story. I believe that the dying process can be a deeply spiritual one, and I think it was for my mom and sister. Being a witness to and a part of their process was a spiritual journey for me as well. I recognize that the spiritual tools I learned since 9/11 equipped me to handle this time of loss and sorrow. After the tragic events of September 11th, I found myself wanting to do my part to help bring more peace into the world. I had found that being an activist or joining a campaign didn't fit with who I was, but I resonated with the idea of doing the inner work to bring more peace within myself and thus to my relationships. I started an inward journey to find more peace within myself at that time. I count this as my first practical application of a recognized spiritual practice.

A few years after that I went through a difficult time in my private life which resulted in my questioning my very identity. I started studying and applying lessons from Rhonda Britten's *Fearless Living* books (and I attended a couple *Fearless Living* seminars). One of the first assignments I did through this program was to write down the things that were missing from my life due to fear. As I reviewed the list, the one item that stuck out in neon to me was "have a spiritual practice." I did not even realize this was something I wanted. I grew up mostly unchurched having attended-very irregularly-some form of protestant church with my mom and sisters until I was about seven years old, and we moved from New Jersey to Illinois. Many years later when I asked her about this time my mom explained that she took us to church just because that is what you were supposed to do, not because she believed in what the church was teaching. Living the Golden Rule and showing us how that was done was the spiritual grounding I received from my upbringing. I am extremely grateful for what my parents taught us in word and deed about caring for one another and I had thought this was enough for me. I thought this was all I needed, so it came as a surprise that I was looking for something more in the way of theology, practice, and community.

I knew that if I wanted to live without fear, which I did, then I needed to answer this call to cultivate a faith system and spiritual practice. At first, I tried to explore eastern religions but, at that time anyway, I found the exploration difficult as the concepts and language were so foreign to me. I thought perhaps New Age was the way to go but at the same time I thought that a lot of the New Age concepts did not fit in with my practical nature. Fortunately, as I did my Google Search for New Age, I found New Thought. The Unity brand of New Thought really caught my attention. I have always appreciated the teachings of Jesus; however, I just didn't resonate with traditional Christian theology. When I read the principles of New Thought, I appreciated the emphasis they put on following the words of Jesus and seeing him as their master teacher. I also liked their acceptance of all people and their belief in our connection with one another. Practicality is important to me as well and Unity has been called Practical Christianity. With some trepidation I found myself attending my first Unity service at Unity of Phoenix. Although I did not understand everything they were saying and some of it seemed very strange, I knew immediately I had found my spiritual home. This is a large church which was perfect for me as I really wanted to engage with the teachings internally before I became involved, and I could do that there. It was a place where I could be a bit anonymous.

Within months of beginning my journey in learning and applying Unity New Thought principles, my sister Karen was diagnosed with stage four breast cancer. During the next two years the Unity principles I was learning and applying helped me get through the time as my dearly loved sister underwent treatment, became a "miracle patient," and finally went through the process we call death when the cancer returned. Attending Unity of Phoenix was an oasis for me. It was a place where I could cry and let go of the pain that watching my sister going through this and then losing her had caused me. I also learned how to apply many of the principles and tools, and that helped me tremendously as well. Finding Unity of Phoenix at that time was a tremendous blessing.

After Karen died, I ended up moving down to Tucson to be closer to my mom. Eventually I found Unity Church of Peace which became Unity Spiritual Center of Peace, Tucson. This was a much smaller community which turned out to be what I was looking for. I knew again that I had found my home. I had just been laid off from my job and found a new job which worked perfectly with their class schedule. I took my practice deeper, and I participated fully in the community as a volunteer and active member. I started taking classes for credit and eventually made the commitment to become a Licensed Unity Teacher (a credentialed leadership position in Unity).

Moving to Tucson, finding the perfect community to deepen my own spiritual practice, getting laid off so my work schedule allowed me to participate fully, and even having my income reduced so that I needed to move in with my mother, all were things that contributed to my being in the right place emotionally, spiritually, and physically during that fateful Joyful Season of Sorrow. Each, often painful step led me to be at the right and perfect place when my Mom and sister got sick. I'm glad I listened to my heart and did what I was called to do so that I could be as present as possible as the events enfolded during the holiday season of 2011. I share our story here in the hopes of inspiring others who may be going through a hard time. I also hope to provide a simple and practical guide on how to apply New Thought principles amidst very difficult circumstances. I now look back at this time and appreciate the opportunity these circumstances gave me to show up and to witness what I would call Love, Order and Good Without Opposite in expression.

I AM

I Am Divine Love.
I Am Whole.
I Am Compassion.
I Am Strength.
I Am Faith.
I Am Gratitude.
I Am Generous.
I Am Grace.
I Am All
All is me.
I Am one with all I see.
All I see is one with me.

There are no True barriers,
Between me and anyone.
We are all eternal.
We are all one.
We can never be separated.
It just can't be done.

I am as close to you now.
Even though you are no longer here physically.
I'm as close to you now.
I feel your love with each breath I take.
I'm as close to you now as I can ever be.
We are one for eternity.
Never to be separated.

You surround me always.
You are the love I see in every person I meet.
You are the love I share each day.
You are the love that fills me with peace and joy.
You are the love that brought me here.
You are the love I have yet to know.

SUSAN J. SMITH

You are my past, present, and future.
I love you so
I know you know.
For we are one for eternity
Love is infinite.
So is our bond.

I am as close to you now as I'll ever be.
Because in Truth
I Am You
You are me.
We are bound together,
By love for all eternity.
By Susan Smith

CHAPTER 1:

CATCH 22

Thanksgiving Day 2011 was a day I am unlikely to ever forget. I woke up in the morning sad and concerned because my sister Sandy, who lived in Phoenix, was not feeling well enough to come to Tucson to spend the holiday with my mother, Jerry, and myself. We would have gone up to Phoenix to be with her but unfortunately my mom woke up the previous Monday feeling very sick herself. She had not felt like she could make the drive to Phoenix. Sandy and I were both single women without children and we were not close in either physical proximity or emotional connection with our extended family. It had been the three of us together for our Thanksgiving celebrations since my sister Karen died on December 1, 2006. It was sad to wake up and know this year we would not be together.

It had been difficult to move beyond those memories of Karen's last Thanksgiving. We had managed, however, to establish new traditions since her passing that had made the day still feel special. It didn't feel right that this Thanksgiving Sandy, Mom, and I would not be together. I was also concerned about Mom and Sandy's health problems. I knew I needed to be home with my mother who was ill even though I wanted to be with Sandy as well.

It had been a difficult week. I was living in my mother's house in Tucson at the time. When I got up to go to work Monday morning (I worked at the nearby Petco part time) my mom informed me that she had fallen out of bed the night before. She said she had had a hard time getting back up into bed and that she had bruised herself when she fell. She was also feeling very weak. She expressed that she felt like this right before she had her heart valve replacement surgery five years before. I could tell she was afraid about what was going on with her body.

I was both concerned about her health and upset that she didn't even attempt to wake me up to help her. She explained to me that she didn't want to disturb me when I asked her why she didn't wake me up when she fell. I did my best to let go of my frustration with her because I knew how stubborn and independent she could be. I hoped that I got the message through to her that I want her to call me if she ever needed help. I explained that it is much more disturbing to me to find out she needed me, and I wasn't there than to have my sleep interrupted. I don't know if she heard me or not. I knew there was no point in holding on to what was already over, so I made my best effort to shift from feeling guilt and anger to forgiveness and compassion.

Unfortunately, she told me about falling and how she felt about half an hour before I had to be at work. Since she had a history of heart problems (arrhythmia plus valve replacement surgery 5 years prior to this) I didn't want to leave her to go to work. I also wasn't sure about what happened when she fell. I didn't see any bruising in the area that she fell on and that was strange as the blood thinners she was taking made her bruise easily. For some reason I didn't think she fell at all. My instincts told me she thought she had fallen and/or perhaps dreamt she had fallen. I will never know what really happened. It was clear that morning that she was weak, and she wasn't her energetic morning self. She was sick and hurt.

A JOYFUL SEASON OF SORROW

She insisted I go to work that day. Where I worked was only a five-minute drive from home so I went in, also there wasn't anything I could do for her. She wouldn't let me take her to go see the doctor or to the emergency room. She promised to be careful and not get up and move around much (not that I could take that promise and put it in the bank). I was very distracted that morning at work. I have a vivid imagination and I regret that I let it run away from me; conjuring up images of my mom falling and not being able to get up. She agreed to let me get her a medical alarm to wear but she wouldn't wear it. I called her when I was on my break. She said she was alright but still complained about weakness. My manager, Tammy, graciously let me go home early after I explained my concerns to her. When I got home my mom said she was better. I was glad I was there, she had a history of being unstable on her feet and I didn't want her to fall again and hurt herself. It was good to be home so I could keep an eye on her.

Throughout the week she felt badly, she even agreed to go to see the doctor on Wednesday, she had an appointment with the Physician's Assistant. After listening to Mom's recitation of various ailments and hearing her describe her fall, the P.A. had a difficult time determining what was wrong with her. She sent her for an x-ray since Mom complained about her lower back hurting. I really thought this had nothing to do with her fall since she had arthritis and sometimes had back pain. They didn't find anything broken on the x-ray. Regretfully, the trip to the doctor and imaging center didn't provide any answers and further exhausted Mom.

During the same week Sandy had gone in for an ultrasound in order to help determine the cause of pain in her back that she had been experiencing with increasing intensity for the last month. She had also been suffering from other health problems. Her doctor's initial diagnosis was Sjogren's syndrome, an autoimmune disease. It can cause anywhere from mild to debilitating symptoms including extreme fatigue, joint pain, and organ malfunction. Sandy had been referred to a rheumatologist. The earliest appointment she could get was in January. The ultrasound was scheduled to check her out for any other possible causes for her health issues. At the point when she went in for the ultrasound Sandy was no longer able to lay on her back because she couldn't get herself up without experiencing excruciating pain. She told the ultrasound technician this. Sandy told me the technician pretty much ignored her concerns. She had her lay down flat. When the test was over, Sandy had to get off the table by herself. Sandy explained that the pain was so intense when she sat up, she almost passed out. The technician then asked if they were checking out other things for her. Sandy found that discouraging because she knew then that the ultrasound probably did not show any reason for her physical pain and discomfort.

Amazingly, Sandy continued to do her volunteer work at Lodestar and worked that Wednesday. Lodestar is a center that provides assistance to homeless people in Phoenix. Sandy had retired from teaching the year before and began working at Lodestar in the fall. She provided GED tutoring and also helped in general in the resource room. When I spoke to her that Wednesday night before Thanksgiving, I could tell that she had had a very difficult day. She was feeling discouraged that she was not receiving any treatment to help her get better. She had been sleeping on a chair for at least a month due to her pain and mobility problems. I had been up twice during that time in order to help her as much as possible (clean house and set up things so they were easier for her). We were quite creative in coming up with a pouring system to feed her dog, TK. She thought it was funny when the food fell on his head when she went to feed him.

It was hard for me to believe it, but at the exact same time my 82-year-old mother and my 55-year-old sister were experiencing serious mysterious medical conditions. Luckily for me I had been a student of Unity New thought teachings for several years prior to this happening. I had an established centered prayer/meditation practice. I was as we say, "All Prayed Up." Being "All Prayed Up" for me meant that even though the ground currently under my feet was shifting in mysterious and frightening ways I could still know the unshakable Truth that Divine Strength, Love and Wisdom were operating in all our lives.

So, it had been a difficult week already by the time Thanksgiving morning rolled around. I had prepared most of our traditional meal already the day before (spaghetti sauce and homemade crescent roll dough). Sandy called and we talked about the Macy Thanksgiving Day Parade with Mom. Mom knew Sandy didn't feel well enough to come home, however, we didn't tell her how badly Sandy felt. I'm afraid, keeping things that might hurt one another, to avoid another's worry or pain, was a Smith family habit. This was Sandy's choice and I honored it to the best of my ability. I eventually took the phone into the other room so I could talk to Sandy privately about how she was feeling.

This is when Sandy told me she was unable to get out of her chair due to the amount of pain she was in. She explained she had gotten up once in the night to use the restroom and that had been extremely difficult. She didn't think she would be able to do that again. She believed that when she got off the table when she had her ultrasound, that she had harmed herself further. I remember being completely shocked when she shared this information with me. I knew I had never felt more helpless. To have someone I loved so dearly be so helpless and, in such pain, and not to be able to be there with her was unimaginable to me. I needed to be at home with Mom who was so weak and needed help getting around. I needed to be with Sandy to help her get the care she needed.

After sharing my distress about this situation with Sandy we talked about her options. If worse came to worse, she was going to call 911 and have the paramedics come take her to the hospital in order to receive treatment. Our good friend Diana Roach lived nearby, and we talked about having her come over to help after she got out of work. At this point, however, Sandy didn't want to take any action as she was hoping she was going to start feeling better. The thing I remember the most about the conversation was the fact that I felt completely at a loss as to what to do. Before we hung up, she promised to call me later to give me an update. She also asked me not to tell Mom what was going on.

After I hung up the phone, I immediately called our friend Diana to see if she could go help Sandy. Diana was at work, so she didn't get the message immediately. I then helped Mom get up and get dressed. This was not help she needed just the week before. She was happy that Sandy called, and we got a chance to talk to her. She was disappointed and a little concerned that Sandy was not feeling well. It was so hard to be in such distress about Sandy's situation and not be able to share my concerns with Mom. In regular circumstance I would probably have overruled Sandy's objection to telling Mom about her health problems, however, since my mom was not at all herself at this point, I felt it would be better for all of us to not burden her with details about Sandy's current circumstances.

I had never before found myself in such a confounding Catch 22 situation. Go to Phoenix to help my dearly loved sister who would do anything for me who, currently was stuck in her chair. Stay in Tucson to be with my dear stubborn Mother who was weak, scared, and may have a heart episode and/or fall down if I left her alone. Little did I know at the time that choices like this one were going to be mine to make for the next six weeks of my life.

Light

Light flows through me,
Light flows out of me,
Light surrounds me,
Light engulfs me.

Light shines on my path.
Making my way and
Each Divine step clear before me.

Light is infinite.
Light is healing.
Light is love.
Light is wisdom.
Light is what we are all made of.

Let there be light.
Creative force of the Universe it is.
Let there be light.
So, I can see the Truth of me.
So, I can see the Truth of you.
So, we can live together in peace.
Knowing that light is who we are now
And for all eternity.

I send light and love
To all the life on the beautiful planet we call earth.

I send light and love
To everyone
To continue to do the work
Of bringing peace and joy to all mankind!

By Susan Smith

CHAPTER 2:
THE ANSWER

I was at a place beyond worry. It was beyond my ego brain capacity to process this horrific family crisis that we were currently playing out. Fortunately, being a student of Unity spirituality, I knew that through meditation and prayer I could access Divine Wisdom and Strength as these are both innate spiritual abilities. Once Mom was settled in the living room, I invested in 15 minutes of Silence and prayer. After centering myself the answer of what to do next came to me. I would drive to Phoenix, pick up Sandy and bring her and her dog TK to Tucson to be with Mom and me!

    I knew immediately this is what I needed to do. I didn't want to leave my mom but I knew that during the 4-5 hours that I would be gone she would be alright. I also knew I couldn't be much help to her if my mind was so preoccupied with concerns about Sandy.

    I immediately called Sandy and told her this plan. She agreed that I should come get her. I told Mom and she also thought it would be good that we would all be together. I gave her more information about Sandy's condition to try to prepare her for when she saw Sandy. She was upset but not nearly as much as she ordinarily would have been. This was just one more indicator that Mom was just not quite herself.

I quickly made sure that Mom was set up for me to leave her and I hit the road. I was glad I had a lot of positive music to listen to as I drove up to Phoenix. I knew I had to be careful and pay attention to my driving. I knew that as the primary care provider I had to stay strong and take care of myself. As I think back on my drive to Phoenix, I realize I relied on my gratitude practice to deal with the stress, worry and fear. For instance, I remembered all that I had to be grateful for. I had the resources, ability, and time to go to Sandy's aid. Mom was well enough so I could leave her home. As weak as Mom was, I knew she would be alright for the time I needed to leave her. I received the guidance I needed when I needed it. I knew that all the Divine Guidance and Strength that I need are available to me at all times. I was grateful to be blessed with the personality characteristics that truly make me happy to serve and help others, especially those that I love the most. I was grateful Sandy called me and told me about her situation.

Using my imagination, I may have been able to recognize the obstacles that were to be on my path in the coming weeks. Fortunately, I have learned about the importance of making progress one baby step at a time. Knowing that each step, however small, will get me and my loved ones where we need to go. Driving to Phoenix was the first step. I didn't even dwell on how I was going to get Sandy to Tucson as I wasn't sure how difficult that would be.

It was with great joy that I drove into Sandy's driveway that morning. I was so happy that I was there to bring her home to be with Mom and me. What a relief to be able to come to her aid.

TK happily greeted me at the door when I arrived. He was always happy to see me, but I think his greeting on this day was even more enthusiastic. He was such a loving animal. I am sure it was hard on him not being able to help Sandy. Sandy was also grateful that I was there, she was still sitting in her chair; however, she said she thought she was doing better. This was always Sandy's way. She always stayed positive and saw improvement even if it wasn't there.

We talked over our concerns about getting her up, getting her to the car, and her managing the ride home. She felt that with my help she would be able to navigate to the bathroom, to the car and in and out of it. After taking care of a few household chores, things she hadn't been able to do herself and she didn't want to leave, we managed to get her up to the bathroom and into the car. She used a walking stick in one hand and put her hand on my back to help steady her. We took tiny steps forward at her pace. I was so inspired by her courage and strength. At the same time, I was alarmed at how difficult this was for her. It was clear that each step was a challenge for her, she was in a great deal of pain.

We were able to set her up in the backseat of the car. Opportunely she wanted to sit in the back since TK suffered from car sickness and only did well if he rode in the front passenger seat. Once we were set up, we called Mom, who was doing alright and informed her we would be home in two hours.

Sandy did really well on the drive to Tucson, she was awake and alert. We actually had fun talking about all the little things we always liked to talk about. We were very close and usually talked to each other every day. We always had a great deal to share with one another, I think we were both so happy to be together. We knew that we would be there for each other through this, we were surprisingly at ease on our trip to Tucson.

As we got closer to Tucson, I discussed with Sandy the option of immediately taking her to the ER. She wanted to hold off and go directly home. She promised if she still felt as bad as in the morning, she would go the next day. Respecting her feelings about this and knowing that we will be with her should she need help I drove us directly to the house. It was a tremendous relief to get home.

Somehow, we managed to get Sandy out of the car and into the house. It was with great happiness that I saw Mom sitting in her favorite chair waiting for us. She was relieved we made it home safely. I remember that I was surprised that she was not more concerned about Sandy's clear pain and problems with mobility, just a week before she would have been beside herself with worry and concern about her daughter. She was happy to have Sandy with us, but she didn't seem to really be able to process the severity of Sandy's condition.

There was one thing that she had been concerned about and that was Thanksgiving Day dinner! I had made the dough for our traditional holiday homemade crescent rolls before I left, but I hadn't rolled any of them out. Somehow, Mom found the strength to roll out ¼ of the dough so we could bake the rolls and have them with our dinner. Considering her physical condition this was an amazing accomplishment. She had to be on her feet to do this. She had to roll out the dough with a rolling pin-something she found painful (due to the mastectomy she had had ten years before) even when she was at her healthiest. It was an act of incredible will for her to have prepared the rolls for us.

At first when I found out she'd gone to so much trouble to make the rolls (and taken the risks) I began to think about how I should have done that before I left. I quickly stopped myself, however, I knew that fleeting thoughts of woulda, coulda, and shouda and their accompanying guilt were likely to occur during this time, however, I also knew that I simply had to shift gears and remind myself that I was doing the best I could under extreme circumstance.

Using the stick and cane method, we got Sandy settled on the other recliner in the living room. Mom was in her favorite recliner and Sandy was in the one next to her. Sandy had me arrange the pillows as best I could so as to increase her comfort. I was so grateful that we were all together. Once she was settled, we had our traditional Thanksgiving dinner, spaghetti with meat sauce and homemade rolls. Mom was very glad she was able to help by preparing the rolls and that we were sharing a traditional meal that night. It turned out to be a surprisingly enjoyable meal. Both Mom and Sandy had appetites and seemed to enjoy the food. I also had an appetite, and my nerves were steady enough that I enjoyed sharing a Thanksgiving meal with my family that day. Fleeting thoughts were coming to mind about what the next day would bring, however, again I chose to redirect my thoughts to focus on all we had to be grateful for in that moment. We had each other, delicious, nutritious food, shelter, friends, resources, and good memories. I believe that I truly was living in the present moment at the time, a practice I know is healing and one I sometimes have difficulty doing under normal circumstances.

That evening we established our sleeping routine. This is the same routine we maintained for the next several weeks. I helped Mom get into her bed. I helped her get dressed and made sure she was settled for the night. Then I helped Sandy with her preparations for bed. She slept on the recliner in the living room since she was not able to lie down and get up comfortably. I would then get myself ready for bed. I slept on the couch in the living room, so I was available if Sandy needed to get up at night. We did develop a cane and walking stick method that seemed to work for her (so she would walk on her own), but she still needed some help since she couldn't bend down. I was also worried about her falling so I would follow her as she walked down the hall. I tried to help get her out of the chair as that was one of the hardest things for her to do. Usually, she wanted to get herself up. She had a system so as to avoid the pain as much as possible. How she managed as well as she did is truly amazing to me. She was a tower of strength and courage. I was so fortunate that both Mom and Sandy taught me so much about dignity and strength in the sight of adversity during these weeks.

Why Ask Why

How did this happen?
How can this be?
Is this some joke the Universe is playing on me?

How did we get here?
What is the purpose?
Why oh why is this happening to me?

Why ask why?
Is what I say.

Why there may be no answer to the question anyway.
Why ask why?
What I need to learn will be made clear eventually.
Why should I question the unfortunate circumstance yet not all the good fortune that has come my way?

Why ask why?
What I really need to know is what is mine to do right now.
Why waste time and energy asking how I got here when I could ask how can I move positively forward?

Why ask why?
What is it with my need to question what has already come to pass?
Why do I drain my energy this way?

Why ask why?
What answer would satisfy me?
Why don't I just accept what is so that I can move forward?

Why ask why?
What authority would be able to provide an answer?
Why can't I just gently remind myself that to release and let go of this question would free me?

Why ask why?
What is the point to this question anyway?
Why don't I decide here and now to shift myself to a more productive question like:
How do I move forward and allow Spirit to guide me?

By Susan Smith

CHAPTER 3:

BLACK FRIDAY IN THE ER

The next morning after I helped Mom get cleaned, dressed, and situated on her chair in the living room I took Sandy to the ER at TMC (Tucson Medical Center). She was able to move about on her own some that morning with the cane and walking stick, however, it was slow going and clearly incredibly painful. She agreed that we needed to get her some help. She only hesitated since she had just had tests done and she didn't want to pay for them again, but she knew we had to seek professional help.

We got to the ER very early (about 6 am). It was Black Friday, so we saw parking lots filled with shoppers and there was a lot of traffic out and about. I had been scheduled to work myself that morning. I knew I had to call in and tell them I would be absent. My family protested this, but I just asked them if they really thought I should work today? They agreed that I was indeed needed at home. When we got to the ER, I went in to borrow a wheelchair. They were so nice they helped Sandy get into the chair and wheeled her right in. I had Sandy's driver's license, insurance card, and credit card with me. She had shown me the day before how she had been carrying these three things in her pocket so she knew where they were should she need them in an emergency. I was so glad that I could now carry these for her. She didn't have to worry about having them in her pants pocket anymore. When she showed me how she had been carrying her identification around just in case of an emergency, I realized how scared and concerned she had been about her physical condition.

I know that both of us felt glad that morning that we were going to get professional help for her. We both had high hopes that they would be able to determine why she was in so much pain and discomfort and that they would offer her some form of treatment.

Everyone at the ER was very professional, providing compassionate and proficient care. Sandy had described her medical history, including the Sjogren's syndrome initial diagnosis and her current symptoms. They did an ultrasound, tested her blood and ran some other tests. At the end the doctors concluded that the diagnosis of Sjogren's syndrome was probably the cause for Sandy's pain. They had given her some pain medicine at the hospital (which we think made her sick) and sent her home with a prescription for pain medicine and instructions to call her physician for follow up.

While we were waiting for the test results, we asked one of the doctors about Mom. We were wondering if they could possibly help her as well. The physician told us some of the things that they could check should Mom come in. We both thought Mom should come to the hospital to be checked out as well (since it was still a holiday weekend, and her doctor was unavailable).

We called Mom to see how she was doing. She was still feeling badly, she was super weak and did not have any energy. We told her how happy we were with the care Sandy was receiving and suggested that I come home to get her and bring her to the ER as well. I knew how very bad she was feeling when she agreed to this. I drove home (about a 30-minute drive) in order to bring Mom to the ER.

The ER was quiet when I brought Mom in. Again, someone helped Mom this time get out of the car and into a wheelchair. She was so weak that it was difficult for her to get up and to move around. Once she was checked in, Mom tried to explain how she was feeling. She started with the story about her fall (which concerned me because I didn't think that was the root cause of her problem). She also explained about feeling very weak. Blood was drawn, tests were ordered, and X-rays were taken to determine the root cause of her health problems.

Now the ER at TMC is large but small enough that I did run into some of the same hospital employees. I certainly caused some confusion as I was going between both Sandy and Mom's rooms that morning. I explained that I was with two separate people which probably is more common in cases where people have been in an accident and/or suffering some form of communicable disease. As I recall, everyone who knew the situation was kind and compassionate to me. I am sure it almost looked like we took a trip to the ER on Black Friday as a family just like we might go shopping in the mall.

It certainly was strange to me. I had never before been in an ER with any member of my family before and here I had both of my family members in the ER at the same time. Life sometimes is stranger than fiction. Little did I know that this was simply a brief preview of what was to come.

Once Mom was settled, Sandy got released. I took her in to see Mom before I drove her home. At the time I think both of our feelings were mixed. On the one hand we were glad that they didn't find something terribly wrong with her and on the other hand we didn't know how long she go could without treatment. At least we had a prescription for the pain pills. We were hoping the medicine would improve her mobility and sleep. I think we also hoped that whatever triggered the intense back pain would heal and mend naturally.

Unfortunately, the pain medicine they gave Sandy caused her to throw up. We figured this was the cause of her nausea since she did not have that problem before we went to the ER. When we got home, I made sure she had what she needed within easy reach. I also tried to make sure she was as comfortable as possible. I was a little concerned about leaving her to go to check on Mom. Sandy assured me she would be fine without me. I am sure she would have liked to have me stay and she knew I needed to go back to the hospital to be with Mom. So back to the hospital I went.

Shortly after I got back to the hospital the ER doctor gave us an update on Mom's condition. He had several concerns. One good thing was they did not find any broken bones from the fall (that didn't surprise me). They had, however, been monitoring her heart and they confirmed that she was suffering from arrhythmia (irregular heart rate). This was a condition she had been treated for ever since her heart surgery. My understanding of this condition was never complete; however, I believe that usually her heart was in sinus rhythm with the occasional episode of arrhythmia. She had a pacemaker installed to help her with this five years ago after her heart valve replacement surgery. It appeared that at this time her heart rhythm problem was more serious than usual. They also found that she was very anemic. The concern was that she may have some bleeding in her stomach. The doctor said both of these issues could be the cause of her extreme weakness. He wanted to admit her so they could get her heart rate under control and to assess the cause of her anemia. He told us his suggestion and mom immediately said, "No, I will not stay in the hospital." He then gave us a few minutes to talk as he went off to take care of another patient.

At this point I was upset that Mom would not take the doctor's advice and allow herself to be admitted to the hospital. As I said she was a woman who knew her own mind (a characteristic that at times I greatly admired). She knew she didn't want to stay in the hospital. I tried to talk to her about how risky it was to have her be so weak at home. I had taken to walking behind her with my arms around her waist to help support her and to "catch" her if she fell, not a very effective technique. I talked to her about my concerns about her falling and seriously hurting herself, her heart, and the need to get it back into the correct rhythm, and the need to identify what was the cause of anemia. She was insistent that she come home. I knew then that it was time to shift gears again. I consciously let go of my fear and frustration and decided to choose to support her decision to come home. Knowing my mom as I did, I knew that in general, she really did not fare well in hospitals. I decided to have faith that taking her home was the best choice at the time.

We discussed that should a problem arise at home that I will have to call the paramedics for help. She agreed that this was alright with her. The doctor came back, and she told him what she had decided. She told him in no uncertain terms that she wanted to go home. He again explained the risks. She was insistent that she be released.

In the end I bought her home. We had instructions to follow up with her primary care doctor and cardiologist. She also had a prescription for potassium which they found out was very low due to her anemia. I was happy that we had the potassium prescription. I remember after her heart surgery she vastly improved after they identified her potassium deficiency. I tried to encourage her and tell her that we were getting closer to figuring out why she felt so weak.

Things Change

Things change.
Yes, things change.
You know it's true.

Things change.
It's inevitable, undeniable,
Without a doubt.
Things change.
Whether we want them to or not.

Things change.
Sometimes for the better.
Sometimes for the worse.

Things change.
People come and go
Traveling through our lives.

Things change.
The physical world is
Designed to be impermanent.

Things change.
My body is a little different now
Than when I first sat down
To write this poem.

Things change.
Sometimes it is this very thought
That gets us through
The tough times we are facing.

A JOYFUL SEASON OF SORROW

Things change.
Sometimes it is this very thought
That scares us into
Clinging to our current life conditions.

Things change.
We can change with them or
We can resist the change.
We can pretend the change isn't happening.
We can hope the change will be in our favor.
We can invest our energy by holding on
as tight as we can to how things are right now.

We can know that things change
In the impermanent world of the relative.
We can know that consciousness is constant
Truth is Absolute.
Principle remains steadfast.
Things change and we can change too
To ever widen our awareness that
Things change but Truth never does!

By Susan Smith

CHAPTER 4:
HOME CARE, HOSPITAL, BIRTHDAYS AND MORE

We all managed pretty well through the rest of the weekend. We all tried to carry on the best we could. We were each learning our roles. I was grateful that Mom and Sandy were together whenever I had to leave home to run a quick errand. Sandy seemed to get a little stronger and became quite adept at getting up and moving independently to a small degree. Mom's condition seemed to ebb and wane. Eventually I learned that nights were the most difficult time for her both physically and cognitively.

    Sandy was more comfortable now that she had pain medicine. She was sleeping quite a bit. Mom was envious of Sandy's ability to sleep. Mom slept more, however, than she thought she did. Sometimes I could interest Mom and/or Sandy into watching a television program or movie. We were heavily into the holiday movie mode already. Mom was not reading, and this was a huge loss for her as that was probably her favorite thing to do. I think we were all hopeful that come Monday everyone's physical condition would improve.

A JOYFUL SEASON OF SORROW

Sunday night came and it was time to get everyone ready for "bed." Mom was really weak as I walked her back to the bedroom. She was also confused and disoriented. She didn't seem to understand what was going on. I learned after this the importance of assessing that mom was mentally alert whenever I helped her get up and move around the house. Unfortunately, one of my biggest concerns, that Mom would fall, and I wouldn't be able to pick her up, became a reality. As I tried to help Mom up off the toilet seat, she slipped off the seat and fell between the toilet seat and the toilet paper roll dispenser. With my assistance we were able to get her out of that uncomfortable position. We continued to work together, and we could not get her off the floor. She was too weak to stand, and I didn't have the strength to get her up either. The good news was that the fall hadn't injured her. The bad news was that she was stuck lying on the bathroom floor.

Helpless is the word to describe how I felt at that moment in time. I was concerned about the fact that I couldn't get her up and into bed. She also seemed to be very out of touch with the reality of the situation. She would respond to me and do what I asked of her; however, her manner was distant, and she seemed to be apart from the situation.

In some ways I was glad that she was not fully cognizant of what was going on. Sandy somehow managed to get herself up out of her chair and into the bedroom (my mom was in the master bathroom) sometime during this crisis. She heard what was going on and knew we were having major problems. Having her there with us at that time was an amazing blessing to me. She helped me brainstorm what we could do to help Mom.

First, we tried to make Mom as comfortable as possible. Then we agreed that we had to call 9-1-1 to get help from the paramedics. We were afraid Mom would resist this, but she actually agreed that we needed the help. She seemed to understand what we were doing at this point.

Like the cavalry, the paramedics came to help us out. I can never emphasize enough how deeply appreciative I was at that moment to be able to call on these kind, compassionate, professional, and talented people to help my mother in her hour of need. Once they assessed that she had not hurt herself when she fell off the toilet seat, they quickly got her up and sitting on the side of the bed. They then did an assessment of her overall condition. They checked her heart rate and discovered she had an irregular heart rhythm. It was also clear that she was confused and disoriented. They suggested strongly that we should go to the hospital. She was not resistant to the idea and consented to being taken to the hospital. I knew that it was the right thing to do at the time. As they got her loaded into the ambulance, I made sure Sandy was set up to be in the house alone. Then I went back to the TMC ER once again. It was about 9:00 pm.

The details of this time in the ER are vague in my memory. I know that X-rays were taken to assure nothing had gotten broken when Mom fell (thank goodness nothing was). Her condition was assessed again as it was on the previous Friday. They discovered she had arrhythmia and anemia. This time, however, she got admitted to the hospital. I stayed with her until she got settled in her room. I was relieved that she was being monitored closely. They had her hooked up to a heart monitor. Once she was settled, I went back home for a rest.

Sandy was glad that Mom got admitted. We both hoped that this hospital visit would help stabilize Mom's condition. Luckily for us, Sandy's condition seemed to have improved, so I was not concerned about leaving her alone (with TK of course) when I went to visit with Mom in the hospital. At this point Sandy was talking about making the arrangements for me to drive her back home. During the next several days I split my time between visiting Mom at the hospital and getting home to Sandy to see to her needs. One thing I made sure of was that Sandy got meals every day.

I honestly don't remember that much about Mom's hospital visit. I know that her anemia got quite severe to the point where they gave her a blood transfusion. They also did a test and determined that she had an ulcer. They thought the ulcer was the cause of the bleeding/anemia. She was given a prescription for an antacid to treat this. They monitored and dealt with her heart arrhythmia while there; however, there was no diagnosis as to why she was having this problem. They just said that to follow up with her cardiologist when she came home. The goal of the hospital visit was simply to stabilize her heart condition and to identify the cause and begin to treat her anemia.

She was in the hospital for four days. One of which was her 82nd birthday. I remembered bringing in a card and a balloon for her that day and making sure everyone knew it was her birthday. I also brought in the cards she received from her friends to share them with her. I was sorry she had to be in the hospital on her birthday since she really disliked being there. Who wants to be in the hospital on their birthday? We both were grateful for the birthday wishes and the special kindness her caretakers showed her that day. Being there on her birthday didn't seem to bother her much. It was being there at all that she was resistant to.

She received physical therapy and seemed to get stronger. This is where I learned the value of a walker. I bought one for both Mom and Sandy before Mom was released. The walkers were called rollators since they had four wheels so that is what we called them. At first it seemed a little wasteful to buy two at the same time, but I thought it would be nice to have one for both of them. Ironically, I told Sandy that if we only needed them while she and Mom were recovering and never used them again, they would be a very good investment.

Having identified what they thought was causing her anemia and having stabilized her heart rate Mom was released to come home with us. With a degree of trepidation that she may fall again, I went forward in faith and brought her home.

I was glad to have her home because I knew it was where she wanted to be, however, I was sorry to lose the security I felt knowing she was in good professional care at the hospital. I was hopeful her condition would continue to improve. It was good for us all to be together again. I imagine those days Mom had been in the hospital had been very lonely days for Sandy.

During Mom's hospitalization Sandy had been busy trying to get an earlier appointment with a rheumatologist. She called her primary care doctor and explained that her condition had worsened to the point that at she had to come to Tucson in order to be cared for. Our hope was that the primary care physician would be able to get her into an earlier appointment, however, they told her they couldn't help her. She tried other rheumatologists and couldn't find an appointment earlier than sometime in mid to late January. She was also paying her bills over the phone and taking care of her business. I tried to help her out as much as I could. As that week progressed her condition started to deteriorate, and it became clear that she was not going to be going home any time soon.

We celebrated both Mom's and my birthday on the following Saturday which was my actual birthdate. Mom had her birthday while she was in the hospital, so we waited to get her home in order to give her her presents. Sandy was always a big birthday person. She had my presents up at her home in Phoenix, so she wrote down what they were on pieces of paper. One was a Camelback backpack that I was to use when we went hiking together. We both became emotional when I opened up that paper and saw what she had bought for me. At the time I don't think either of us could imagine a time when she would be feeling well enough to go on a short walk let alone a hike with me. One of our presents to Mom was tickets to go to the play, *White Christmas* in a couple weeks. We decided not to give the tickets to her since we thought it was likely that we would not be able to go to the show together. I got pizza and cake for the celebration, and we watched a movie together. Both Mom and Sandy were able to enjoy some of the food so that was good. It was a difficult day in many ways. I was glad we did our best to make it special.

God Is Neutral

God is here.
God is there.
God is everywhere.

God is neutral.
God is love.
God is good all the time.

God doesn't bestow special blessings on anyone.
God doesn't decide what's right or wrong.
God is light.
God is Principle.
God is the same all the time.

God is always here, there and everywhere.
The presence of the Universal Divine Power
Is obscured by human error consciousness of
Violence, Lack and Loss.
Yet by simply taking a deep breath
We can bring our connection back to the Truth Principle
There is not a place where God is not.

Just as 2 plus 2 doesn't recognize the error
When we say the sum is twenty or twenty thousand.
The one great absolute positive
Force of Infinite possibility
Does not recognize error
Whether it be an angry word said or
An unimaginable act of horrific terror.

Just as 2 plus 2 always equals 4
No matter how many times we
Get the answer right or wrong.
Divine Principle is ever the same
No matter by how much

SUSAN J. SMITH

We miss the mark of
Absolute perfection.

We were made in the image and likeness of Spirit.
As such we are by birthright
Creators of our universe.
We create the world we live in through our
Thoughts, words, and deeds.
It is through our Divine creative capacity,
Conscious awareness serving as our guide,
We continue to move forward.
Getting ever closer to living lives that
Demonstrate the Truth
That our birthright is Divine love, Divine Peace and Divine wholeness.
Our job is to make choices.
To live ever more closer to the
Truth of each of our own Divine Nature.

By Susan Smith

CHAPTER FIVE:
TRY AND TRY AGAIN

The next couple of weeks we all did our best to carry on. We had some low points, and we had some high points. Reflecting on those days, my strongest memory is that of hope and persistence in light of ever worsening conditions.

Sadly, Mom's health and strength declined rapidly after we got her home from the hospital. Somehow, I managed to get her to her follow up doctor's visit. When the doctor saw how weak she was, she wanted to place her in a rehabilitation nursing home so she could get physical therapy. She was surprised that I had even managed to get Mom to the appointment by myself. She was hoping that arrangements could be made for the rehabilitation center to pick Mom up from her office. Surprisingly Mom agreed to this idea without any protest. Eventually I took Mom home hoping that arrangements would be made for her to be admitted to a rehabilitation center so that she would get the care and the therapy she needed in order to get stronger. We heard back from the doctor's office that afternoon that Mom's insurance would not cover a stay at a rehab center. Instead, arrangements were made to have some in-home physical therapy for her. At first, I was disappointed that we were unable to follow the doctor's recommendation, however, since Sandy's needs at the time were becoming more pronounced, I thought perhaps this solution was for the best.

I remember having some difficulty getting Mom back into the car after our appointment. Mom was using the walker at the time to get around. Walking from the doctor's office to the car took almost more strength than she had. Getting herself seated in the car and her legs in the car was another challenge altogether. I tried to help and support her as much as I could, I remember helping her lift her legs and getting them in position in the car and making sure she had her seat belt on. As I was helping her, I was saying encouraging words about her efforts to get in the seat and about the opportunity before her to receive physical therapy in order to increase her strength. Truthfully, I was saying these things not just for her benefit, but to keep myself from giving in to fear and worry about the immediate and future challenges before us.

Just as we finished getting her settled a woman who was getting in the car next to us, said how beautiful it was to see the care I was giving to Mom. She explained that she had experience working in health care and she was moved to see the loving interaction between Mom and myself. At the time I realized how kind words from a stranger can give one a boost just when we need it most. She was definitely one of the angels I encountered during this time.

Mom started on her physical and occupational therapy the following week (about 1 ½ weeks after her hospital stay). The therapists were two more angels that helped us out during this time. They first did assessments. Then began doing exercises with Mom and left homework for her to do. Having their kind professional help was a huge lift for all of us. Just knowing that we were taking steps to improve the situation was a lifeline for us. Mom was so good with them and always did what they asked of her. I really encouraged her regularly to do her homework exercises (sometimes with more success than others).

The paramedics that came to our aid during this period were all angels as well. The weekend after Mom was released from the hospital while getting her ready for bed, I had my arms around her waist when she began to slide to the floor onto her bottom. I was able to stop her from falling by balancing her weight on my knees; however, I didn't have the strength to boost her back up. She eventually, therefore, slid down on the floor first on me and then on her bottom. Sandy had some mobility at this point. She quickly realized I would not be able get Mom up again, so we called 9-1-1. Help was there before we knew it. The paramedics quickly got her up and seated on her rollator. We thanked them for their kind help and sent them on their way. We should have had them put Mom on the bed because after I rolled her to the bed, I realized she didn't have the strength and I was unable to lift her up and position her in bed. After a bit of deliberation, we called in the Cavalry again. The paramedics came and they quickly got her positioned in bed. I have to say that I was embarrassed to have to call them back again. I explained that she had just been released from the hospital and she had been stronger when she was sent home. By and large they were really nice, and their help meant everything to all of us at the time. I went to bed (couch) that night hoping that Mom would be much stronger in the morning and that whatever was causing her extreme physical weakness would pass.

One really good thing was that once Mom was in bed for the night she never needed to get back up until morning. That was a tremendous help since her mobility and cognitive ability became so limited at night.

Although I regretted the fact that the reason Sandy was with us was due to her failing health, there was a silver lining in having her in Tucson with us. Although I did the physical work, we were a true team as far as figuring out what to do in order to help Mom out as much as we could during this time of apparent rapid decline. One thing we determined was that the three times we had to call the paramedics to help Mom were during times when I was helping Mom prepare and get into bed. Each time she was not mentally alert and aware. At both incidents she seemed confused, and this mental state seemed to add to the physical weakness she was experiencing. So, Sandy and I agreed I would not help her move around should she be in this confused state. This meant some nights we all ended up sleeping in the living room. Mom and

Sandy would sleep in their recliners, and I would sleep on the couch. TK was always on the floor nearby. I know that by coming up with this system we avoided some problems.

Problem solving, making the most of what is before us, and creative thinking were all characteristics of how our family functioned in a crisis. I was so grateful for the fact that we were taught how to handle challenging circumstances. Sandy and I were in full problem-solving crisis mode during this entire time. I think between the two of us we tried to think of everything we could do in order to make everyone comfortable and stronger physically.

For example, Sandy was very concerned about losing strength and muscle tone due to the fact that she was sitting 99% of the time. Once we had the walker, we would go out for very short walks around the block if she was up to it. It was important to her to push herself to do this. I also thought it was important for her to get out of the house some. One time, to get them both out, we all loaded into the car, not an easy task, to go for a ride. Going for rides was something Mom loved to do after her heart surgery. This ride, unfortunately, was not successful. We drove for about five minutes and Mom was ready to go home. Sandy was perfectly happy to go home as well. It was disappointing that they did not enjoy the ride. I was glad, however, that they were willing to give it a try.

Sandy continued to try to get an earlier doctor appointment. She also contacted her doctor about her pain medication. She was concerned about taking a strong narcotic regularly for over a month. Her physician prescribed a high dose ibuprofen for her to take instead. I tried to respect her decisions although at times I was frustrated because I thought the stronger pain medicine would have offered her more relief than the ibuprofen.

While we were in this seemingly interminable waiting pattern, I started researching Sjogren's syndrome to see what could be done to ease Sandy's discomfort. I went to the Sjogren's syndrome website and read information there. I also purchased the book they suggested about the disease. Due to this research, we discovered that her symptoms should be reduced by eating anti-inflammatory foods. Through an internet search I found anti-inflammatory foods and recipes. I bought cherries and made a special Gorp for her. I bought avocados, as an activity we made guacamole together. She was having some digestion issues, so I also bought foods that she wanted to try and that sounded appealing to her. I don't think we felt like any of these things made a difference and we kept trying one baby step at a time. These actions made us feel less helpless.

My mom was also having issues with her diet. Her appetite had been in decline some for the last several months, however, by this time her appetite was seemingly non-existent. She didn't even want her Sees birthday candy and she was a major chocaholic! I offered to pick up anything that she wanted to eat. I did manage to entice her to eat a snickers bar and a couple of ice cream bars. I could get her to eat a few bites of some of her favorites now and then. I got creative and made her an Ensure milkshake to try to coax her to get her nutrition from the Ensure. My biggest success of all was the food I picked up from KFC. They both ate the food I got from there. That was a good moment.

Mom listened to me and tried to eat just like she tried to do her physical therapy. She just wasn't herself at this point. She was always committed and generally a really good patient, wanting to do what she could to get better. I tried to encourage her with both her therapy and her diet without nagging or complaining.

Shopping for products that would make life easier and more comfortable for everyone became one of my pastimes. I was grateful that I could leave Sandy and Mom for short periods of time in order to pick up what we needed. They had each other and knew they could call me. During those few weeks in December, I purchased two rollators, a heating pad for Sandy's back (which I ended up using more for Mom). I bought diapers and hygiene products for Mom to alleviate concern should she need the restroom and have mobility issues at the time. Sandy suggested this idea and it was tremendously helpful. After the paramedics came that one night, I bought a transportation wheelchair to use in times when Mom was too weak to walk. I bought easy on and off sweatpants for Mom. Gum and special mouth rinse were bought for Sandy's dry mouth symptoms. I purchased a bed rail and physical therapy belt in order to help with Mom's mobility issues. I went out and purchased anything we could think of that might ease the situation. At the time I was very appreciative that we had the financial means to acquire these tools that we used to make our situation the best it could be. I became quite familiar with the medical supply store and the medical supply aisle in Walgreens. Each time I brought something new home I had such hope and optimism that it would be just what we needed. Many of the things were indeed very helpful.

During this time, I did try to care for myself as well. I would usually be the first person up in the morning and I would do my WII fit exercises then. I tried to eat regularly as well. Investing time in silence and in prayer when I found it also kept me grounded. I knew that it was important that I stay strong since I was the primary caretaker for both Sandy and Mom. I find it incredible that I stayed healthy and physically fit during this whole time.

I certainly did have some low times mentally. Shortly after coming home from the hospital, for instance, Mom would begin each day asking how long it would be before she would die. This was so unlike her, and it completely took me off guard. Whenever she asked this, I would tell her she would get stronger. She just needed to eat and do her exercises. This was never an easy conversation to have, and we had it at least once a day. Now I understand that she knew her system was shutting down in a way that only she could know. She was telling what she knew in her heart to be true. She was in the process of dying. At the time it was a baffling and sad conversation for me since I felt I was doing all I physically could to help her to get stronger and better. She also went through a period when she complained about being in severe pain. She had a high tolerance for pain, so this was really unusual for her. She never even took any pain medicine when she came home from the hospital from her open-heart surgery. She took Tylenol regularly for arthritis pain. I helped her as much as I could with her pain. I gave her the medicine. I applied the heating pad to the source of her pain. I put a topical pain reliever on it. Still, she would complain. I called her primary care doctor to see if they could do anything for her. They said I would have to bring her in for an appointment in order to get help for the pain. We had a follow up appointment scheduled for the cardiologist already that week. I knew that another doctor's appointment would be too much. I told them I would call back. I was glad at least that we had a few remedies to try that did give her some relief.

Somehow, we managed to make it to the cardiologist appointment. Getting Mom in and out of the car was incredibly difficult but working together, we did it. She really had cause to complain as when I tried to help her move her legs and body into the passenger seat, I would hurt her on accident. She was very patient and appreciative of my efforts to help her. We went to see the cardiologist during her second week home from the hospital. Her doctor immediately identified that Mom was suffering from arrhythmia. He felt that the arrhythmia was why she was feeling so weak. He gave her a prescription to help her and told her she would feel better quickly. She seemed skeptical and I was hopeful about this new medicine.

Our trip to the cardiologist was challenging as well because I found it difficult to leave Sandy. Sandy was starting to have problems keeping her food down. I helped her with that before we left for the appointment. I didn't want to leave her; she had also become hypersensitive to light and noise. When Mom and I watched television, we used subtitles and the TV Ears so as to not disturb Sandy. Sandy also took to wearing sunglasses in the house so that the light would not bother her eyes. The rapid decline of her condition scared me. She wanted to see if some of the things we were trying would help before I took her back to the hospital. I was hopeful and I knew that a second trip to the ER was probably in our future.

After she started taking her new medicine that the cardiologist prescribed and receiving Physical and Occupational Therapy, Mom's condition improved. Sandy's continued to get worse and worse. It was getting to the point that Sandy was unable to keep any food and/or liquids down. This went on for a couple of days. I started talking to Sandy about getting her back to the hospital. She wanted to try one more thing. For a 24-hour period she didn't eat or drink anything except water. We both knew that when she was not able to keep water down, we had to get her back to the hospital for help.

Metaphysical Malpractice

I feel I am to blame somehow for what is occurring.
I feel I am to blame because of the quality of my thinking.
What we think about multiples and attracts us to what we desire.
What we focus on expands.
Knowing these laws, I had to ask:
How could my subconscious want more of this pain and suffering?

I'm afraid to look inside my head.
How could my thoughts be so negative,
To bring about these sad tragic circumstances?
I'm afraid to find out that somehow, I brought all this loss upon myself.

If mind action is always at work,
How did my thoughts manifest a set of circumstances that are my worst nightmare?

As these words rush about and condemn my consciousness,
A gently voice is heard about the din.
It has two words for me,
It whispers:
Metaphysical malpractice.

With this gentle reminder,
A whisper so calm and peaceful.
I was able to hear it,
Above the noise of anger and confusion.
By its very gentle nature this voice caught my attention.

Metaphysical malpractice.
That is what I've been doing each time I blame myself or the quality of my thinking
For the circumstances that I find myself in.

Metaphysical malpractice.
It was good to know that I wasn't to blame.

SUSAN J. SMITH

Neither was anyone else.
Circumstance come,
Circumstances go,
It's not up to me to question why or wherefore.
It's up to me to
See, know, think and be the best I can be.
Notwithstanding the circumstances I happen to be in.

My spiritual tools help me to do this.
With my tool chest at the ready,
I can mold and shape the circumstances to be a life experience of
my choosing.

I vow to myself that now and in the future.
When my adverse ego blames negative circumstance that befall me on the quality of my thinking.
I will remember that circumstances come and go.
I will do my best to mold my experiences.
I will remember not to indulge in metaphysical malpractice.

By Susan Smith

CHAPTER SIX:

THE LONGEST NIGHT

I ended up taking Sandy to the ER on the evening of December 17th. Knowing that this trip to the hospital was likely to happen, I had tried to find someone to come and stay with Mom, however, I did not have any success. Before I took Sandy to the hospital, at about 8:00 pm I helped Mom get into bed and made sure she was set up for the night. I left her rollator next to the bed (it had her water, tissue, and other supplies on it so she could reach them). I put a note on it reminding her I was at the hospital with Sandy and in big letters I wrote, "Don't Get Up." Since she had been sleeping through the night and hadn't been getting up, I thought she would be fine.

Driving to the hospital that night little did I know that the longest night of my life was ahead of me. I had no idea that within 15 days both my mom and Sandy would be admitted to the hospital, be diagnosed with end stage terminal cancer, would be admitted to hospice, and would pass away from this physical life they were sharing with me. Life as I knew it was about to change irrevocably and completely.

When we got to the ER at TMC I went in to borrow a wheelchair. Fortunately, the ER wasn't crowded, and they took Sandy in right away to be examined. I don't think she could have waited. Her condition was very severe. Our first experience that evening with the ER staff was the only somewhat negative one we had. When the admitting nurse asked Sandy what her symptoms were, Sandy explained that she was there because she was vomiting on a regular basis even though she hadn't eaten anything. The admitting nurse asked the right questions and on the surface, she was professional, and both of us got the impression that she didn't think Sandy really needed to be there. This made Sandy feel even worse. We talked about this after she was settled in a bed. I empathized with Sandy because I got the same impression, but I told her not to pay attention to it. We had to get some medical help for her. She could not continue on the way she was. Left unsaid we both knew that her very survival was at stake at this point. Although our perceived attitude of the receiving nurse put us both off, she did ensure that Sandy got admitted immediately and received the fast medical attention she needed. I suggested that we should just be grateful that the nurse did this vital part of her job perfectly for us.

While we were there, the doctors and nurses did their assessments. They took blood samples and ran some tests. They did what they could to make her comfortable. I felt better just being there. I didn't think that her condition could be ignored any further. I think Sandy was glad to be there and anxious to get professional medical help.

After an hour or two the doctor came in to tell us the results of Sandy's tests. He told us that her vomiting problem was being caused by an excess of calcium in her system. He was admitting her so that they could find out what was causing this problem and to get it under control. He had compared the bloodwork from her visit a few weeks prior and that helped him ascertain the situation. That made me glad we had gone on what at the time, had seemed a somewhat pointless ER visit. This was another good reminder that we don't always know the outcome of and reason for things that we do and/or happen to us.

The doctor was incredibly kind and compassionate. He took the time to explain that he wasn't admitting Sandy because he was a nice guy, and he wanted to help her to stop throwing up, he was admitting her because of her condition. He didn't know what was wrong. The next day when I heard the nurses say renal failure, I realized he was preparing us for the severity of Sandy's condition. I believe we were subconsciously aware of how sick she was at this point but hopeful that what was wrong with her body could still be put right.

I sat with her a while wanting to be with her when she was admitted to her hospital room. We were both so grateful that she was finally getting professional help. I didn't want to leave her until I knew what room she was going to be in. I don't know why this was important to me, but it was. As we were waiting for her to be moved to her room, we overheard the medical personnel's conversations with the patient in the bed next to Sandy. This patient was an elderly woman that had a large cut on her arm. The unusual thing was that she didn't know how she got the cut. They kept asking her how she cut herself and she said she didn't know. Her confusion made me think of Mom. I decided and Sandy agreed, I should get home to check on her (we didn't want to call and wake her up). I told Sandy I didn't want to leave before I knew she had a room. Fortunately, the kind nurse heard this and told me he had a room number for her. I got the room number from the nurse then I gave Sandy a kiss and drove back home. My primary feelings at this point were relief and faith that it was alright. I chose not to give in to despair and worry as I saw no point to those emotions.

The minute I got into the house I called out telling Mom, "I'm home!" I wanted to tell her that Sandy was now getting the help she needed. I went to Mom's bedroom. To my complete shock and dismay, she was not in her bed. She wasn't in her bathroom. I couldn't believe that my worst nightmare was coming true. I found her in the guest bathroom, the one we used because we could fit her walker in it. How she got there I have no idea. She was lying on her back on the floor. Her pants were bundled around her knees. Her hair was wet. Her eyes were open and yet she seemed to look through me. I asked her, "What happened? Why did you get up?" She answered in a very faint voice, "Stuck."

It was hard for me to figure out what had happened. Had she hurt herself when she fell? How did she get wet? I felt so guilty about leaving her alone. I called 9-1-1. I waited by her side. I think I was suffering from shock myself. I know I was trying to understand why she got up. She had protection on, so she didn't have to get up to use the bathroom. Why didn't she read the "Don't get up" sign? Why did I leave her walker right by her bed for her to use?

The paramedics came to our rescue again. Never before had we needed them this badly. I explained to them that I got home at 12:30 am and found her on the floor. I said that I had taken my sister to the hospital at 8:00 pm. When I got home, I found my mom in the bathroom. She could have fallen anytime between 8 pm and 12:30 am. I felt really useless, and I don't think I was very coherent when I spoke to them.

There was some concern that she had injured her back in the fall. It was determined, however, that was not the case. Once they decided her back was not injured, they quickly got her up off the floor and into her transportation chair. She was conscious and yet not verbally responding to questions. It was like she was in another world. We got her out of her wet cold clothes. One of the paramedics had me put an Afghan in the dryer for a few minutes so it was nice and warm when we wrapped her up with it. While they were examining her, I was hugging her. I was telling her how much I loved her. I apologized for leaving her. There was no doubt she needed to go to the hospital. Her heart rate was irregular, we needed to see if she had broken anything in her fall, and she was mentally dissociated. All of these issues needed to be addressed at the hospital. As they went to get the gurney in from the ambulance, they saw the second walker and asked what it was for. I explained that was the walker my sister used to get to the car when I took her to the hospital.

A JOYFUL SEASON OF SORROW

As they prepared Mom to go to the hospital, I got our dog TK situated. Poor TK, I am sure this had been a hard night for him. He was a very loving animal. It was 1-1:30 when they took her to the hospital. I was able to drive right behind the ambulance. I will never forget seeing her head bopping back and forth as she was seated on the gurney in the ambulance. She looked out seeming to just stare into space.

I could never have imagined that I would be taking another family member to the hospital on this night/now morning. At the time I was simply going through the motions. I was taking things one step at a time. I never would have believed that although it was very traumatic getting my mom into the hospital on the same morning that Sandy was admitted, would prove to be the most optimal situation considering the circumstance we all found ourselves in. I was no longer equipped to care for each of them on my own. We all needed to be there to get the physical and emotional help we needed. Also, it was much easier for me to have both of my family members in the same building so that I could support and care for them. We also needed information about what was really wrong with both of them.

Forgiveness

Sometimes I question myself.
Am I doing all I can to help you through your time of challenge?

Sometimes I question myself.
Am I being kind and compassionate as I see as best I can to your needs?

Sometimes I question myself.
Am I overlooking something that would miraculously cure you?

Sometimes I question myself:
Am I up to the task that has been set before me?
Perhaps someone else would do a better job helping you?

Sometimes I question myself:
Am I using my time wisely?
Am I expecting too much from you?
Am I pushing you enough to do for yourself what you can?
Am I doing all I can to help you?
Am I doing more than I should?
Am I asking the right questions?
Am I asking too many questions?
Am I using the resources available to us?
Am I ever going to be done with this endless task of taking care of you?

Sometimes I forgive myself when I question anything I've thought, said or done.
No matter the outcome I know my love for you is more than enough.
I know you wouldn't want me to beat myself up because sometimes I think I should be better that I am.

I forgive myself when I need to.
I forgive you when I need to.
I know that in letting go, forgiving the error,
I have room for the love and compassion to heal and guide me forward on the adventure of care taking that I am on.

By Susan Smith

CHAPTER SEVEN:
BLESSING IN DISGUISE

Once we got to the hospital, it seemed Mom was less responsive than before we took her in. She didn't in anyway recognize me when I met her in her ER room. It was then that I saw the small bump on her head. Mom was put into a private room in the ER. They immediately began monitoring her heart. The nurse gave her medicine to get her heart rate under control (it worked for a little while!). The same doctor who cared for Sandy took care of Mom. I had to explain to everyone who recognized me in the ER that yes, I am back with my mom now and I just left here a couple hours ago. Since Mom was taking blood thinners the doctor said we needed to have a brain CT done when he saw she had a bruise on her forehead. We had just noticed the bruise when we got Mom to the hospital, and they were wheeling her bed into her ER room.

They let me go with Mom while she went to get her CT scan. I really appreciated being with her since she seemed so lost and alone. I wanted to be as near to her as I could while she was clearly not able to think for herself. I was even able to go into the room with her. The technicians were so incredibly kind and did all they could to make her comfortable. When they were ready to start the test, they let me sit in the room with them so I could keep an eye on my mom during her scan. Fortunately, the test didn't take long. I remember before we left the technician wished me luck. That was a little unnerving. We had talked a bit about Mom and her condition, and the technician had been very kind. I took her words for the encouragement they were meant to be, even though a part of me thought maybe there was something on the test that she saw that was of concern.

As we were waiting to go to back to the room after the CT scan Mom asked a question that made sense! She suddenly seemed to recognize me as well. She wasn't completely coherent and yet she was vastly improved in awareness. The nurse who was with us when this happened asked Mom "Where have you been?" I explained to Mom we were in the hospital because she had fallen and hurt herself. She didn't remember what had happened to her (she never did remember which I think was just as well).

Mom eventually got resettled in her ER room. She was much more aware but still not talking much. I did what I could to make her comfortable. Eventually the doctor came in (the same doctor that had seen Sandy earlier). He explained that Mom did have a small bleed in her brain as a result of her fall. Since she was on the blood thinners, they could not operate to stop the bleed. All they could do was admit her to the neurology ward for observation. A neurologist would then check on her progress. I don't know how much of this Mom understood.

When he was done talking the doctor took me out to the hall to talk. His kindness will always be remembered by me. First, he asked me if I would like a hug. I accepted the offer. At the time I was reeling over the fact that Mom might have become fatally injured due to the fact that I left her alone that night. The doctor then explained to me that there was no way to know how severe her injury was. He did let me know that it had the potential to be life threatening. Considering her mental state, I was very concerned that she may have suffered from some form of brain damage due to the fall. She was also so fragile. The tenuousness of her mortality was very real to me at the time.

A JOYFUL SEASON OF SORROW

When I was explaining Mom's accident, I had shared with the doctor that she had fallen when I left her alone in order to take Sandy to the hospital. I told him this because I wanted him to know why I didn't know what happened or when she fell. After he went over the potential severity of her condition, he asked me about her resuscitation orders. He explained how he had requested a DNR order for his own father a short while ago. He knew how difficult that was to do; however, sometimes it was the best choice. I knew Mom's wishes in this area, so I told him to change her orders to DNR. This was a harder choice to make than I expected it to be. Less than a month before my mom had been active, alert, and independent. I didn't want her to miss out on good quality years of her life if that could be avoided. Also, as her heart was clearly not functioning properly, a Do Not Resuscitate order seemed especially significant.

When the doctor brought this up, he kindly said that I should not blame myself for what had happened to Mom. He said he could see the guilt and the self-recrimination in my eyes. He said I had already done so much for my family that night. How wonderful for a busy ER doctor to take the time to minister treatment to my wounded heart and soul that morning. His words helped bolster me up. I went ahead and told him to place a DNR order on Mom's chart. Fortunately, I had Mom's medical power of attorney and living will at home just in case I should need it.

The next several hours passed in a blur. I remember the next nurse who took on Mom as a patient said supportive words about Mom being a DNR patient. That was helpful. I remember sitting by Mom's side watching the machines. We were waiting for a bed in neurology. The nurses came in regularly and did neurological tests on Mom. They did all they could to keep her comfortable. She was aware I was there and yet she really wasn't completely aware. I did tell her Sandy had been admitted and that I would visit her soon to give her an update. Since Mom's condition seemed so tenuous at the time, I stayed close by her side. When the night was done the new ER doctor came in to check on Mom. The main thing I remember about her was that she said very matter of factly, that Mom was having a heart attack! She didn't seem too concerned about it though. They just kept monitoring Mom's heart as they had been doing all along. She said they were waiting for a bed and a request had been made to Mom's cardiologist and a neurologist to check on her condition. Mom would be moved once a bed opened up in neurology. We had been waiting about eight hours when I realized it might be a while longer before Mom was settled in a room. She seemed more stable by the time morning came. I gave the nurse my cell phone number and went to visit Sandy (to check on her and give her an update about Mom).

Sitting by my mom during those hours I amazingly was able to release the guilt and regret I felt about leaving her alone and coming home to find that she had fallen and injured herself. During those hours, due to what I can only call through the power of grace I also let go of the frustration I had with my mom for getting up. I also released most of the frustration I had over the series of events that led us all to that moment. In regard to forgiving myself, I realized this might have happened if I had been home and she failed to wake me up (like the first night when she had fallen). It was also possible, I realized, that she could have fallen and laid there a while even if someone else had been in the house with her. I was very aware that with all the challenges facing all of us there was no energy to spare on the selfish pursuit of guilt, anger, and remorse. I felt a tremendous sense of grace and peace amidst the most challenging set of circumstances I have ever found myself in.

Having largely dealt with any regrets on my part about what had happened, I felt prepared to go to Sandy's room to tell her about Mom. TMC is a large hospital, so I felt very successful when I located Sandy's room (being directional challenged that is). I was glad that I had not gone to see her immediately after I brought Mom to the hospital since Mom's condition on the surface, anyway, had improved immensely from when she we first brought her to the hospital. I was grateful that I found Sandy in her room. I was concerned that she may have been out for some tests. I was so glad that she was in a hospital where she was finally getting the help she needed so badly.

A JOYFUL SEASON OF SORROW

When I first saw her, I asked her how she was doing. She explained that the hospital doctor had been in and that she was scheduled for many tests that day. She seemed upbeat and grateful that the doctors were working to get to the bottom of what was causing her problems. She said the nurses had been kind. It seemed that everything that could be done was being done to keep her comfortable. She was still battling nausea.

After we spoke about her situation, I explained to her that Mom was brought into the hospital after I got home the night before. I assured her that Mom had already stabilized a great deal and that she was in the ER waiting for a room in the neurology ward. I told her what had happened. I also explained the doctor's concern about the brain bleed. She agreed with me that neither of us should feel guilty about what had happened. There was no point. We just needed to move on and do what we had to do. Talking to her made me feel so much better. I hope I told her how much help she was to me during that time. Her strength in dealing with the pain, fear, and challenge of her own illness, let alone her support and help in dealing with Mom's situation gave me the boost I needed especially after the past twelve hours or so spent at the hospital.

We both agreed that having both Mom and her in the hospital at the same time would make my life easier. It would have been so much harder to have one or the other of them in the hospital and one at home now that they both were having so much difficulty. We were sorry that Mom went through such a hard time the night before and we agreed that the fact that this event got Mom back into the hospital was a blessing in disguise.

The rest of that day I went between Mom's ER room and Sandy's room. Sandy had a lot of X-rays and scans done that day. Sometimes I would go by her room, and she would be out. From what she shared with me it was an extremely difficult day for her. Mom was being monitored in the ER. Finally, after about 18 hours in the ER she was transferred to her room in neurology. At some point I went home, took a nap, fed the dog, and showered. I also took a few minutes to pray. As I prayed, I set the intention that I would always know where to be and when I would need to be there in order to support my family. I knew this whole situation was way beyond what my ego brain could handle. This was my chance to let Spirit take the lead, while appreciating my ego's ability to assure that I stayed organized and able to function. I consciously chose to allow instinct, the voice inside, to guide me now that I found myself in a situation where control, logic, and reason would cause a symphony of terror in my thoughts and actions. I had never before experienced such a clear set of circumstances in which I needed to let go and let God (universe, Divine Mind).

I was glad I took a few hours to take care of my needs. It's amazing how a short rest, brief investment in prayer and a shower rejuvenated me. I was also glad I had the time to take care of TK. This was important to all of us. When I got home, I quickly put the house back together so as to not have to face the evidence of a night that I am unlikely to ever forget. Once I felt rejuvenated, I was anxious to get back to the hospital to check on everybody.

I had told Mom that Sandy had been admitted. Mom still wasn't thinking that clearly, but I think she was glad to know that Sandy wasn't home alone and that she was getting the care she needed.

Having set the intention to just allow the Truth to guide me in knowing where I needed to be, I was able to relax and focus on doing what I could at the time, where I was. I also made sure the nurses had my cell phone number so they could call me should Mom or Sandy need me. I had explained to them that I had two patients that I was taking care of at the hospital, at the same time. The nurses and all the staff on both wards were very helpful and supportive. I was very appreciative of the love and care they gave my family. Having both of them sick at the same time meant that not only was I torn between helping each of them, but they also were unable to support each other.

Mom was finally moved into her room in neurology that afternoon. She had a single room and received careful monitoring as a patient on this unit. I think each nurse and aide had only 3-4 patients since they were the ones who did the neurological monitoring on this ward. Having her monitored so closely was another one of those blessings in disguise.

Sandy had had a long first day in the hospital, she underwent an extensive series of tests. I remember being in her room when the nurse shift change came. As the one nurse explained to the other information about Sandy's care and condition, words like "renal failure" caused me to realize that Sandy's condition was more serious than we thought.

All in all, that night I went to bed so grateful that both Mom and Sandy were in capable hands. I was really hopeful that more information about both of their conditions would be discovered soon so that they could receive the treatment they needed in order to get better.

Need to Know

I understood that to let go of my need to know,
Is what I needed to do,
In order to know what I needed to do.

Letting go of my need to know,
What was to become of all of us.

Letting go of my need to know,
If I can do enough to help.

Letting go of my need to know,
If I was doing the right thing.

Letting go of my need to know,
How we were going to handle the challenges before us.

Letting go of my need to know,
Who to blame and hold responsible.

Letting go of my need to know,
Why these challenges were all happening at once.

Letting go of my need to know,
If I did indeed have the strength to get through one more hour with so much pain in it.

By consciously letting go,
Unbelievable as it seemed to my personality,
I could see the outworking of Divine Order in our lives.
Even when everything seemed to be in chaos.

By consciously letting go.
Unbelievable as it seemed to my personality,
I recognized the unexpected blessings that were outcomes of these events.
Events that I never would have chosen to have happen.

A JOYFUL SEASON OF SORROW

By consciously letting go,
Unbelievable as it seemed to my personality,
Allowing my faith in Divine Guidance to steer the course,
I look back without regret at what I said and did during those days that mightily tried me.
By consciously letting go,
My reservoir of strength was never ending.

By Susan Smith

CHAPTER EIGHT:

WE ARE ONE

I woke up the next day refreshed after getting some much-needed rest. I remember I stopped by the store and bought Sandy flowers for her room (Mom didn't like cut flowers). When I parked my car in the hospital lot the only space available was located next to a car that had a "Respond With Love" bumper sticker. These bumper stickers had been passed out at my church one day after services. Every car I ever saw that had one of these stickers belonged to someone in my community. That was a nice sign that I was being guided and supported. I was grateful that both Mom and Sandy were in the N.E. section of the hospital making it easier to spread my visiting time between them. Not surprisingly (due to my directionally challenged nature) when I went to visit Sandy, I turned down the wrong side of the unit. Just as I was getting ready to turn, I saw Cindy Cawthorne, a friend and teacher from the Unity church I attend. This was rather remarkable since at the time our community was very small. She was visiting her father who was suffering from pneumonia. It was so nice to see her and to get a hug from her. It was a reminder of my wonderful supportive Unity family. I know it was no accident that I took that wrong turn that morning.

Sandy was awake when I came in, she loved her flowers. It was good to see the smile on her face when she saw them. Several doctors had been in to visit her already. She had visits from the kidney doctors, they were working on getting her calcium numbers under control. They said that her nausea would stop once that improved. She also learned that she had several broken bones in her back, and these were causing some of her intense pain. More tests were ordered and treatment options for these broken bones were discussed with her. She was also undergoing more diagnostic tests so they could determine the root cause of her medical problems. The hospital doctor who was overseeing her case asked her if she got her annual mammograms and colonoscopies done regularly. Ironically, she had just missed her mammogram appointment because she was in Tucson and not up to making her appointment in Phoenix. Since he brought up these tests, we realized a cancer diagnosis was a real possibility. We both tried to stay positive, however, it was becoming clear that she had a serious condition. We were both still hopeful that once the cause was determined that she would start treatment and get better.

The news from Mom's doctors was more encouraging. Mom was becoming more aware and cognitively able. She was consistently passing the hourly neurology test she was given. The brain bleed was still a reality but the threat it may cause seemed to become much less of a concern. She was still suffering from incredible weakness and had no appetite. Hospital food made it even more difficult to encourage her to eat. There was nothing that I suggested to bring to her that seemed to entice her at all.

She did ask about Sandy. Having heard about all the doctor's reports I realized I needed to prepare her for what may be coming. I told her that Sandy's condition was serious. I assured her that Sandy was getting the best care possible. Sadly, due to Mom's weakness and close monitoring, and Sandy's broken back and mobility issues, they were not able to visit each other in their rooms (at least on that day). Mom's main comment about the situation was, "How did this happen to us?"

Interestingly Mom didn't complain about her pain anymore. Otherwise, her behavior and physical status were similar to what it had been like before she had gone into the hospital. She was a very sweet patient. She always expressed appreciation to the nurses, aides, and other hospital staff when they came in to help her and to see to her needs. The only time she got impatient was with the people who came to draw her blood. Mom had had a mastectomy on her right breast. This meant that all IV's and blood draws had to be done out of her left arm. Her veins were small and difficult to find. The hematologist would often have to come back to try again and/or have the supervisor come to draw her blood. By the end of the week her entire arm was black and blue. The hematologists were very kind. I hope none of them took her frustration personally. She never would have wanted the people helping her to feel bad. It was just that the whole process began to understandably wear at her.

By the end of the day first full day on the neurological ward I had felt confident Mom's condition was starting to stabilize, at least regards to the neurological aspect. She did still exhibit confusion, but this was not a new behavior and I thought it was unrelated. At the same time, we were very uncertain about Sandy's condition. Sandy had been worn out from all the tests that she was put through. Considering her condition, I am not sure how she got through it all. She was incredibly brave and strong. Just as she had been all my life, she was a wonderful role model to me about strength in the face of unimaginable challenges. That night Sandy and I talked about how unreal the situation seemed. I joked that it was like we were trapped in a bad Hallmark Christmas movie. The ones that are so depressing and seem so improbable (like the one where the boy buys his dying Mom shoes for Christmas). Fortunately, being able to see humor in whatever situation we found ourselves in has always been a helpful coping mechanism for our family.

The next morning, I tried to get to the hospital early in order to be around when the doctors came and did their rounds. I always started off visiting

Sandy. Since Sandy was out for so many tests and Mom was so fragile and confused, I spent more of my time with her. That morning I brought in my Star Wars snowflake poster for Sandy. A friend had made Star Wars snowflakes for me last year and I had put them on a poster. I hung it up on Sandy's wall. I was hoping that when people came to Sandy's room, they would see it and it would make them smile, of course, I thought Sandy would like it as well.

The good news with Sandy was that the treatment for her high calcium levels was working. She wasn't experiencing nausea or vomiting anymore. The renal doctors were pleased with her progress in this area. She had also had doctors in telling her what they could do to repair her broken bones. She did not seem enthused at all about the procedures they were suggesting. Also, they were still running more tests to determine what was at the root cause of her health problems.

That morning she expected the hospital doctor to be by to give her an update about her overall condition. Since he had mentioned cancer, I wanted to be with her when he came in. There was no way to know when he would be in so she told me she would call me when he came. Overall, she was tired and weak that morning. All the testing, etc. seemed to wear her out. I also know she was scared about what the doctor was going to share.

She assured me that the hospital staff was taking good care of her. She did complain some about the aide who cared for her the night before. Sandy said this aide was going on and on about how she was going to have a miserable Christmas since she was single and didn't have a boyfriend. I was glad Sandy shared this with me so she could vent a little bit. She thought the aide's attitude was rude and inconsiderate. I thought the aide's behavior was downright unintentionally cruel. To complain about your upcoming Christmas to a very sick hospital patient, someone who may very well likely be in the hospital for Christmas and was suffering so much like Sandy, was unconscionable to me. We both hoped Sandy would not have that aide help her again. The truth was, this person was an exception, the nurses, aides, and all the hospital staff were all very kind and considerate to both Sandy and my mom. We agreed that we wouldn't give this aide more power by dwelling on her negative attitude.

After a brief visit with Sandy, I went to check on Mom. I told Sandy I would be back to give her a report about Mom when I could. Mom was happy to see me. Fortunately, since Mom was still confused about things, I was with Mom when the neurologist came by. The neurologist had good news. Mom's brain bleed was under control. It stayed small and did not pose a threat to her any longer. Now the doctor's main concern was about Mom becoming strong enough to leave the hospital. I was very relieved by this report and somewhat concerned about the idea of taking Mom home in her condition. I didn't want her to come home only to fall and hurt herself again. I was also worried about dividing my time between being with Sandy at the hospital and with Mom at home. The doctors were aware of Mom's weakness and knew that she needed to be stronger before they sent her home. They left her on the neurology ward and ordered physical therapy for her. As far as her heart condition went, the plan was to have it managed in the hospital and then have the cardiologist follow up with her treatment when she got home.

I was so happy to be able to go to Sandy's room to give her the good news about Mom. She was also relieved that the danger from the brain bleed had passed. After I shared that information with her, she told me the hospital doctor had been in to see her. She said she tried to call me, but it got confusing for her and he didn't have time to wait so he had already talked to her.

She started off by telling me that the news was bad. Again, the doctor had started off by asking her if she had mammograms regularly and colonoscopies. He then explained that she had cancer, she had cancer of the bone and in several of her organs. He told her he had made arrangements to have an oncologist come to talk to her about her treatment options. He also made the arrangements to have a biopsy done on her lymph nodes. I remember when Sandy told me this she said, "I'm sorry..." Even in light of such terrible news about her personal health, she was thinking about what this would mean to me. I remember being completely shocked. All the evidence had been pointing to her being seriously ill; however, I still couldn't believe it. I know I assured her that it was not her fault that she was so sick and there was no need to be sorry. She had done all she could to get help and find out what was wrong with her. After telling me this terrible news she asked me to get her a milk shake.

Before I got the milkshake, I invested a few moments in silence and prayer in the wonderful chapel they have at the hospital. This news was beyond my comprehension. As I sat in silence the words to a Daniel Nahmod song titled "I Don't Need to Know," from his *One Power* CD (Nahmod 2022) came to my mind and comforted me. The words to this song came to mind many times in the upcoming weeks. During this time spent in prayer, I set the intention to know that it is not I, but the Christ within that does the work. I reaffirmed my knowledge that I have the strength and the will to do and be what I need to do and be in order to support my sister and Mom at this time.

I then went and got the milkshake from the special drink stand they have at the hospital. The lady who made the milkshake for me was very kind. She went out of her way to make just what I ordered even though it wasn't on the menu. I remember thinking at the time I was experiencing one of those moments when I was looking around wondering how the rest of the world all seems so normal when my own world seems to have been turned on its head.

When I got back to Sandy's room, I told her that I was in shock and couldn't believe this was happening. She said she understood how I felt and that is why she sent me to go get the milkshake. She wanted me to have a chance to take a walk and be on my own. She was, as always, the big sister looking after me. We then talked about what the doctor told her. We didn't know what to make of the diagnosis. We were glad, however, that we did have some answers about what was wrong. We were hopeful that the oncologist would offer a treatment option that would increase the quality of Sandy's life and extend it as well. Sandy was slated to have numerous more diagnostic tests that day.

As I left Sandy's room, I realized that I needed to decide what to tell Mom. In my opinion, Mom needed to know what was going on. She needed to know because Sandy needed me, and this would affect what I could do for Mom. Also, she needed to know because she had a right to know what was happening to her daughter whether she understood it or not. Since they only had a few patients, I got to know Mom's nurses and aides pretty well. I remember when I went in to visit with Mom, after I found out about Sandy, I told the nurse about Sandy's diagnosis. I just wanted them to know what was happening since it affected Mom. Also, it was good to share with others what was happening. These caregivers responded to this news with great kindness and compassion. When I saw Mom, I told her Sandy's condition was serious. I decided to wait to learn more before I gave her details. In addition, at the time I told her, she wasn't very present. I was hoping to find a time when she was stronger and more aware when I gave her more details.

That day I spoke to the social worker about Mom's release. It was clear that even under the best of circumstances I would not have been able to care for Mom at home upon her release. Luckily, the doctors understood this and were referring Mom to a rehabilitation nursing home prior to returning home. The social worker gave me a list of places that Mom was eligible to go to. I was to get back to her the next morning with my top three choices. She also said that I would have to transport Mom myself since her insurance did not cover transportation from the hospital to the rehabilitation center.

When I went home that afternoon, I called some friends to inquire about the rehabilitation centers on the list. I felt that feedback about their firsthand experience would help me select my top three choices. The social worker said I could set up tours of the facilities, however, I knew that would prove to be very difficult to arrange. When I called my friends, I shared with them briefly what was happening with both Mom, and Sandy. My one friend, Marcia, suggested that we contact Hospice ourselves to see what services they could offer Sandy. The hospital doctor had set up an appointment with the palliative care nurse, but we really didn't know what that meant. I appreciated Marcia's suggestion. There was no reason we couldn't look into this ourselves. Through the help of my friends, I had my list of the top three places for Mom. I also picked up a few things at Target to help with the transport. I bought some easy to slip on shoes and sweatpants for Mom to wear. At least I could make that part of the process easier. I also bought Sandy a cute snowman pillow that she could hug.

That afternoon I got back just in time to meet the oncologist and hear what she had to say. She was a very kind and compassionate doctor. Sandy really liked her. The doctor thought that Sandy's cancer probably started in her breast. She explained how doctors run all types of tests and yet they fail to check the breast for lumps. She did a breast exam and confirmed Sandy had breast cancer. She felt that she would be able to offer Sandy treatment that would enhance her life and extend it, this sounded promising to us. The biopsy was scheduled for the next day. She explained that the information from the biopsy would help her determine the best treatment. I remember her asking Sandy about whether she drank or smoked (Sandy didn't do either) and she said that it was always the good ones that got cancer. She was impressed with Sandy's strength and courage.

I agreed with her that Sandy was so courageous. She was also weaker than she was when I first brought her to the hospital. I know that at this point her energy was lagging. They were still doing a lot of tests and examinations in order to determine treatment options for her broken back bones, etc. She was getting exhausted. It seemed like her physical condition was deteriorating rapidly. She chose to have the biopsy the next day but then she said she wanted to be done with diagnostic tests. We talked about calling Hospice ourselves at this point. She decided she wanted to wait to see what the palliative care nurse had to say to us.

That afternoon Mom seemed to be pretty much the same. I was happy that she stopped complaining about pain. I didn't like to see her suffering. She did get up a few times with the help of two of the hospital employees to sit in the chair to eat. She watched some television; however, she really couldn't follow any plots or conversation. I tried to find animal/nature shows for her to watch. It was a relief to know that she would be getting some physical therapy when she was moved to the nursing facility since she was so very weak.

I was so grateful that I had TK to come home to that night. He was a very calming presence to me. After a bit of both good and very bad news, a day of important decisions, an emotional day where my world was turned upside down, I was very grateful to be able to come home and to get a good night's sleep. I consciously reminded myself not to worry about what would come next. I was moving ahead one step at a time

I'm Alright, I'm Fine

I'm alright.
I'm fine.
Don't worry about leaving me behind.

I'm alright.
I'm fine.
Our bond is eternal.
I have faith and know this Truth in my heart.
I'm alright.
I'm fine.
I'll miss you so.
I know this is true as well.
I'll miss you so.
I know that also
In truth you can never leave me.

I'm alright.
I'm fine.
The future doesn't scare me.
I'll go forward one step at a time.
I know others have done this and I can too.
I'm alright.

I'm fine.
I wish you peace and rest.
I would never bond you to me
When I know it's time for you
To lay your physical body to rest.

SUSAN J. SMITH

I'm alright.
I'm fine.
My future may seem uncertain and lonely right now.
I know I'll be alright.
I have years of loving memories
To keep me company.

I'm alright.
I'm fine.
Go on to do what is next for you.
I am strong.
I have support.
Most importantly I have faith and know that we can never truly be parted.

By Susan Smith

CHAPTER NINE:

DECISIONS

I arrived at the hospital early the next morning. Sandy wanted me to trim her nails and give her a sponge bath before her biopsy operation. I felt bad that I didn't think to help her more with these things before. When Mom and Sandy were home, we had shower days during which I helped them both shower (we had a shower chair in the one bathroom) but once they got to the hospital, I didn't think to help them with their hygiene. I brought some things from home to use to help groom Sandy. I had even purchased a shampoo cap as well, but I didn't get a chance to give her the shampoo. She was tiring really easily, and she needed some rest in order to deal with the operation ahead of her.

I gave her the snowman pillow and told her that I took TK shopping at Target, and he picked it out just for her. He wanted her to think of him every time she hugged the pillow. She liked the story and seemed glad to have her new stuffed friend. He came to be called Best Bud.

Sandy had her biopsy surgery that morning. I didn't get a chance to meet her doctor or hear from them firsthand how it went. I waited in the surgical waiting room during her surgery, so they knew I was there in case they needed a family member. I also waited there so that I would be sure to know when the surgery was completed. The surgery ended up taking longer than expected. There was also some mix up about where Sandy was sent for recovery. Overall, the communication I received about her surgery was incomplete and at times incorrect. I found the confusion and lack of communication somewhat frustrating at the time. I also knew, however, to put my frustration in perspective in regard to all that was happening, and to remember that everyone at the hospital was doing their best for us. I didn't let the mix ups in communication about the surgery cause me much additional stress.

In addition to the surgery this was an eventful day for Sandy and Mom. I don't remember the chronology of what happened. I do remember being where I needed to be when I needed to be throughout the course of the day. At some point Sandy and I spoke to both the palliative care nurse and the TMC Hospice admitting nurses. The palliative care nurse gave us valuable information about receiving end of life care. She also gave us suggestions about how to talk to the oncologist about Sandy's prognosis. At this point we had questions for the doctor. We wanted to know the doctor's opinion about what kind of time and/or quality of life Sandy could expect in the future. The hospice nurses talked about the treatment Sandy would receive and the support we would get as a family from TMC Hospice. Sandy had pretty much chosen the hospice option; however, she still was not ready to commit. So, we made an appointment with TMC Hospice nurse again for the next day.

Sometime during that day, I told Mom that Sandy had end stage cancer. I wanted her to know that Sandy was having the biopsy done. Also, Sandy's condition was getting worse and worse rapidly. I knew I couldn't wait for Mom to be stronger in order to talk to her about Sandy's serious health problems. Some people may question my choice to talk to Mom about this. I felt that she deserved to know, and I did not have the right to keep this information from her simply because she was not in a position to know and was weak and sick herself. Also, for selfish reasons it helped me to know that, however she reacted, that I could share my pain and sadness about this with her. Mom was shocked when I told her. The one thing I remember her saying was that I had told her it was serious. When she said that, I realized that perhaps she understood more about what was going on than I thought.

Mom's low blood count had again become a serious concern. They had given her a blood transfusion the night before. Due to her anemia, her release had been postponed. She was scheduled to have a colonoscopy the next day in order to, hopefully, identify the source of her blood loss. I didn't think that much about the test or what the results might be since between the two of them so many X-rays, scans, and tests had been done without any conclusive results. At the time I was honestly relieved to know that Mom's hospital stay was prolonged since we were clearly at a critical juncture in regard to Sandy's condition.

That afternoon Sandy and I agreed that it was time to make some calls to those that were closest to her to advise them of her condition. This had all come up so fast and she was not home, so most people close to her were completely unaware of what was going on. We planned to call people the next day (we would have called them that afternoon, but I didn't have their numbers with me). I knew it was important that we do this soon. Although no one told us this, I knew that Sandy was slipping away very fast. Time was running short.

By that evening Sandy had resolved that she wanted to become a hospice patient. She was so tired of the testing and monitoring. She had one more bone scan scheduled that night and then she was done. I remember thinking that I wanted to honor and support her decision. I was very tired when I got home from the hospital that night. Sandy called from the hospital at about midnight. She was anxious and wanted to talk. I don't remember much of what was said as I was half asleep at the time. I know now that she was scared. I talked to her for a little while. I am not sure why I didn't just go to the hospital when she called. At the same time, I know that maybe I needed a good night's sleep in order to be able to cope with the next couple of days. I know there is no point in beating myself up over this. I was doing the best I could at the time and hindsight is twenty twenty.

Circle of Love

Love comes in
A never-ending flow.
It's part of me,
It's part of you,
It's part of everything,
We see,
We do.

Love comes in
It fills me with joy and peace.

Love comes in,
Sometimes I close my eyes to see
This beautiful sight.

Love comes in
It's ever present.

Love comes in
It can never be outside of me.
Love is who I Am.
Love is eternal.
Love is never lost.
Love is never separated from me.

Love is here,
All the time,
Whether I recognize it or not.

Love is here.
I close my eyes,
Dream about the Truth of this.
I relax in this thought for a little while.

A JOYFUL SEASON OF SORROW

Love is here.
It never leaves.
It's in the air I breathe.
It's in the food I drink.
It's in the earth itself.

It's in all nature's bounty.
It's in the ingenuity of human design.
It's in my hopes and dreams.
It's in my very mind.

I breathe in, I breathe out.
I know the love that resides inside.
The love that I Am is the conduit,
To embracing all the love there is.

Love flows most freely when,
I know it is who I Am,
I know it is never lost,
I know it is all around,
I know it is infinite,
There is more than enough,
To fill everyone to overflowing.

The overflow I share.
There is no fear in this.
The infinite supply is always there.
No lack shall I experience.

The love flows in
It becomes one with me.
Love is my true identity.
The love flows out and joins
In the one love that fills us all,
Every single pore of our beings.

By Susan Smith

CHAPTER 10:

SURREAL

I went to visit Sandy in her room when I got to the hospital the next morning. She wasn't there. That gave me quite a start. Fortunately, before I could ask, I was told that Sandy had been moved to a private room across the hallway. Sandy was not doing well that morning. Her breathing was much labored (they had her on oxygen). She told me she had a difficult night, so the nurse had her moved to a private room. Also, at Sandy's request the nurse had gotten paper for Sandy so she could write goodbye letters to give to her loved ones after she was gone. She gave me the letters she wrote to me, Mom, Joe, Judy, and to her friends. I carefully tucked them away so I had them when the sad occasion arose when she was no longer around, and I would need them. The nurse also promised Sandy they would make arrangements for Mom to visit her the next day.

    She was very clear that morning that she wanted to become a hospice patient. We already had the appointment with the hospice nurses later that day. She was concerned about talking to the oncologist about her choice (we didn't see her the day before) because she didn't want her to feel that she didn't appreciate the doctor's efforts. I assured Sandy that the doctor was so kind that she would be very understanding of her decision. I was grateful that the hospice nurses were able to work around my schedule that day so I could be with Sandy when she filled out the paperwork to enroll. Mom had her colonoscopy that day and I wanted to be with her when she went for this test.

When I saw Mom that morning, they were having her drink a huge quantity of "go lightly" in order to cleanse her system. I think she had been up a lot that night, so she was not very alert. It was a relief when they came to take her for the test so she could stop drinking that liquid. I think she was very patient with the whole process. I know I would have been frustrated if someone was trying to get me to drink several gallons (or so it seemed to be) of liquid in a few hours' time.

I went with Mom when she had her colonoscopy. I was grateful because I was able to sit with her in the preparation/recovery room. I only had to wait a short while until the actual test was completed. Truthfully, I didn't think they would find anything wrong. I just thought this was one more standard test that would not provide any valuable information.

I was very wrong. Once Mom was back in the recovery room the doctor came in to speak to us. He told us that he had bad news. Mom had rectal cancer. He showed me the pictures and I could see she had a very large tumor. That tumor was causing her bleeding. I don't think Mom understood what he was saying. I was again, in shock. At the same time, it was good to have some explanation about what was going on with Mom's body. Everything that had been going on with her now made so much sense to me.

I remember going back with Mom to her room and telling the nurse about the diagnosis. She gave me a much-needed laugh when she said, "Where do you live?" in response to the news. She seemed to be implying that our problems came because of our environment (like we lived in Love Canal or something). Her honest response just hit me as very funny at that moment. In retrospect it doesn't seem funny to me as living in a place that causes cancer really isn't funny. I hugged and thanked her for making me laugh. While Mom was recovering and not fully conscious, I went to tell Sandy about Mom's diagnosis. Sandy's first response was to tell me that she felt bad that she couldn't be of more help to me with Mom. She had always thought that should the day come that Mom needed us we would care for her together. She agreed with me that it is best that we finally understood what was going on with Mom. I shared with her the laugh I had with the nurse.

When Mom was better, the complex arrangements were made for her to visit Sandy. Mom was hooked up to heart monitoring machines, so she had to have a nurse and a transport person with her. This wasn't convenient to manage. I was in Sandy's room with her when the scheduled visit was to take place. I remember we were both so excited about the visit. At one point I went into the hall to see if she was coming. I saw her coming down the hall and I told Sandy, "She's coming!"

Sandy did most of the talking during the visit. She told Mom how much she loved her and about how grateful she was that she was her mom. She listed many of the wonderful things Mom did for us when we were growing up and what they meant to her. Mom took Sandy's hand. She just kept saying, "How did this happen to us?" I stayed quiet and tried to let them have their moment together. I imagine that this whole scene had an emotional impact on the hospital employees that had to be in the room to monitor Mom. I was very happy that they made these arrangements for them to see each other. It was so important to all of us. The nurses really went out of their way to make sure this happened.

Sometime that day Sandy and I made a number of difficult phone calls. I dialed and spoke first explaining that I was with Sandy, and we had very bad news to share. Then I told the person about Sandy's health. I then gave the phone to Sandy so she could talk to them herself. Her breathing was getting more labored by the minute, so it was a good thing I was there to help her make these calls. It was physically difficult for her to talk. This was probably one of the hardest things I have ever had to do. We gave everyone my phone number so they could contact me about plans to visit. Seeing her rapid deterioration,

A JOYFUL SEASON OF SORROW

I advised them to come as soon as possible. This wasn't easy for any of them since we were two hours away from where most of them lived (and remember it was Christmas week). Sandy's oldest and dearest friend, Judy, made plans to fly in from Denver on Christmas Eve to visit and help out. There were some people that we did not get a chance to contact that I know would have liked to have talked to Sandy. If we had time and the contact information, I am sure we would have contacted more people; however, it just wasn't to be. These are the people that I would be calling in a couple weeks. We did the best we could under worsening conditions.

We did have our appointment with TMC hospice that afternoon and arrangements were made for Sandy to be transferred to the onsite hospice facility, Peppi's House the next day. Sandy's choice to become a hospice patient also changed the treatment she was receiving. The focus of her care became seeing to her comfort rather than on testing and treatment. Sandy felt confident in her decision, and I supported her 100%.

I was so glad I was with Sandy when the oncologist visited. Sandy explained to her that she had chosen to be a hospice patient. The doctor completely understood. She also said that if Sandy's condition had been as bad as it is now, she would not have suggested any type of treatment. This confirmed my concern about Sandy's rapid decline. When I walked out of the room with the oncologist, she remarked about how brave Sandy was. She was right. Sandy was so brave. Her bravery helped me to be brave as well.

I spent the night trying to sleep on a chair in Sandy's room. One of my mom's best friends and neighbors was taking care of TK for us. That was a tremendous help. That night one of my mom's nurses came to me in Sandy's room in the middle of the night for a signature so they could take Mom for some test. She knew I was there in Sandy's room. I always told them where I would be in case they needed me. Something about seeing her walk into Sandy's dark room in the middle of the night for my signature for something to do with Mom was so unreal. It brought home the whole surreal quality of this experience.

The next day we got our usual early start. It had been an uncomfortable night. Sandy and I both laughed about the trouble I had sleeping in the chair. I didn't seem to have enough weight to keep the back down, it kept sneaking back up on me. Even so, I was so appreciative that I had been able to spend the night sleeping in Sandy's room. It meant a lot to both of us to be together that night. At least we both got some sleep anyway. I knew it would be another eventful day so any rest we could get was appreciated.

This Moment

This moment is a sacred time.
It's all I have, and it is everything there is,
All at the same time.

This moment is a sacred time.
I breathe in and appreciate it.
There is no yesterday or tomorrow,
As long as I remember
To treasure this beautiful moment and all the grace within it.

This moment is a sacred time.
All the knowledge of the Universe is at my command.
All I have to do is ask and what I need to know is within me.

This moment is a sacred time.
I'm so glad I get to share it with you.
It is a joy to be beside you and bask in your beautiful presence.

This moment is a sacred time.
Every word, laugh, look, and touch we exchange means so much to me.
Our moments in this physical world are finite.
There will come a day all too soon,
When we will be parted physically.

This moment is a sacred time.
Every moment of my life
Is sacred and divine.
I remind myself now and again,
This moment is a sacred time,
When I start to forget to treasure the moment before me I am so fortunate to experience

By Susan Smith

CHAPTER 11:

PEPPI'S HOUSE OR THE BAHAMAS?

Sandy's condition seemed worse than it had been the night before. It was difficult for her to talk, and her breathing was even more labored. They had her on a high level of oxygen (I could hear the hiss very clearly). That morning she had a kind of anxiety attack, the nurse and the aide were in the room at the time. They did all they could to help her. I will never forget the kindness and love they shared with her while they worked to help her calm down. The nurse held her hand and had her take a few deep breaths in order to calm down. They also put a cold compress on her forehead. I was gently massaging her leg with my hand. I stayed with her until she started to feel better.

I knew that it was a matter of time before she transitioned. I could tell it would be happening soon. Knowing this before I left her that morning, I told her that if it was time for her to leave that she should go. I assured her she didn't have to wait for me to be with her physically in order for her to leave. I told her that I knew that no matter what I was always with her, and we would be together. She asked me if everything was OK between the two of us and I told her everything was fine between us. There were no words or feelings that were left unsaid between us. I felt more at ease leaving her knowing that we had that conversation.

Mom was sitting up eating her breakfast that morning when I came in. She seemed alert and aware. It gave me hope that she would have some quality time left. She was sitting in her chair when the surgeon came to talk to us about a treatment plan for her rectal cancer. The surgeon began by telling us about this very intense complicated surgery that he was planning to do to treat Mom's cancer. He also explained that Mom would have to go through extensive tests to see if her body, especially her heart, was strong enough to endure the surgery. Mom was pretty alert at the time; however, I don't think she understood much of what he said. Thankfully, Mom had always been very clear about what her medical wishes were should she be unable to choose for herself. She had told me she wouldn't even have breast surgery again should her breast cancer return. I knew that there was no way she would want to have this invasive and dangerous surgery.

After the doctor finished speaking, I asked him about what options were available if Mom did not choose to have the surgery. He explained that she would then be eligible to be a hospice patient. At this point I simplified the situation for Mom explaining the options were surgery or hospice. She clearly said she did not want surgery. I also knew that under more aware times this would have been her choice. Interestingly the doctor was relieved when we told him that Mom did not want the surgery.

Once Mom expressed the desire to be a hospice patient, her care changed as well. Her black and blue arm was no longer getting stuck with needles. The monitoring they had her on was less intensive. The biggest change was that I stopped trying to get her to eat and drink. The nurses were all now focused on providing comfort for her. It was interesting to see the switch in both Mom, and Sandy's care when they became hospice patients. I remember there was something that one of the doctors had ordered for Mom that the nurses did not allow to have done, saying she was now a hospice patient. I will always be thankful for them standing up for Mom and saving her the discomfort by making sure this wasn't done.

Sometime in my interaction with the hospice nurses and social workers, arrangements were made to have Mom admitted to TMC Hospice and transferred to Peppi's House as soon as possible. I think we had our first meeting that day sometime. I was so grateful that both Mom and Sandy were going to Peppi's House first. This would give me time to make the arrangements at the house to bring them home. Although it was becoming apparent that Sandy probably was not going to be coming home at all.

Sandy had some visitors that morning. I felt better leaving her in order to take care of Mom since she had people to visit with. I know it was hard for them to see her and realize how bad off she was. Her breathing was very bad, she was getting a rattle in her breath which I knew could mean the end was near. I am very appreciative to those friends that came from Phoenix to visit.

Also, Sandy managed to arrange one more visit with Mom. Again, Mom was wheeled into Sandy's room by hospital staff. This second visit was similar to the first one. It was harder because I knew that Sandy was saying goodbye to our mom. I think Mom knew that as well. This was the second daughter my mom had to face probably dying before her. I can't even begin to imagine how hard this all was on her.

That afternoon Sandy had a couple more visitors. The principal, Darlene, at the school Sandy last taught at, Holmes Elementary School in Mesa, AZ, and her friend came to Tucson to visit. I am so glad they came. Darlene talked to Sandy about all the lives she touched in her years working as a gifted and inspiring educator. Darlene took the time to express her gratitude and appreciation to Sandy and all the wonderful work she had done during her career. Sandy had a big life and touched so many, she deserved to have someone recognize this. My conversations with Sandy were more about how much she had meant to me as a big sister, best friend, and a daughter to Mom. I was grateful that she heard this recognition for the impact she made in the world during her life that day.

We were expecting Sandy to get transferred to Peppi's House that afternoon. Sandy was a bit anxious about the pain she would endure during the transfer. Peppi's House is a building located on the hospital grounds and she would have to take a van ride to get there. The hospice nurse provided the doctor's orders for the move and assured that the floor nurses took care of everything prior to the move. I know that Sandy was excited about getting out of her hospital room.

Darlene and her friend were with us when the lady came to transport Sandy. They helped me gather up her stuff (flowers, Best Bud, hospital stuff) to transport to her new room. I rode in the van with Sandy, and they followed us. I was thankful for whatever they gave Sandy as she was peaceful and not in pain during the ride. What a relief that was. Once Sandy was settled and was resting peacefully, I had Darlene drive me back to the main hospital. I did a quick check on Mom and assured her that Sandy was settled. Mom seemed so much more peaceful to me that night. She wasn't hooked up to machines anymore. She wasn't getting stuck in the arm anymore for blood draws. As hard as the situation was, I was so grateful that they were both resting peacefully and getting the care they needed so as to ensure their comfort. I went home to check on TK and get a few things to spend the night with Sandy.

The room in Peppi's House was very nice. She had her own room, there was a door to an outside patio area. There was artwork on the walls, a couch, a cabinet with the TV. It felt much more like home. One of the things I liked best was the quiet. Except for the oxygen she was receiving, the room was devoid of hospital noise. It was an oasis. Sandy had been sleeping so deeply when I left her, I was completely surprised to see her alert and awake when I arrived back in her room. She asked me where I had been. I didn't feel bad that she had missed me. I was glad she was so alert and realized I hadn't been around. She was so happy to see me.

She started immediately telling me how much she loved her room and Peppi's House. She said she could imagine that she was anywhere in the world, and she has chosen to be in the Bahamas. She had such a great attitude and seemed to be feeling better. It was fabulous to see her so peaceful. The nurses and aides that came in were so kind. They had given Sandy a nice spa treatment. Her hair was clean and brushed, etc. I know this made her feel good. They gave us both apple juice and we toasted being there and that Sandy felt up to drinking the apple juice. At one point someone mentioned that there were CDs that we could listen to. Sandy wanted to listen to Glen Campbell music. We always listened to Glen Campbell music at Christmas. This was a long-held family tradition. Probably brought about the year Sandy got a Glen Campbell album for Christmas and played it over and over and over. This is how she always played her music. They didn't have Glen Campbell and that was alright. We laughed again about our funny Christmas music tradition.

Sandy and I enjoyed being together that night. I think I was more at ease in general knowing with absolute certainty that both Mom and Sandy were getting the care they needed. I think I was able to let go of the stress and strain that all the uncertainty about their health and how I could help them had been causing. I was pretty tired that night (I didn't sleep much in that funny chair the night before). Since Sandy was still awake, I laid on her bed opposite her. I had my feet at her head and her feet were at my head. We talked about silly things that night like the funny songs we listened to growing up. Like "MacArthur Park" and the funny metaphor of leaving the cake out in the rain. Eventually we were both ready to sleep. I slept on the couch. Sandy rested very peacefully that night, she seemed so at ease there. Her only concern came when they told her they were going to come in and turn her on her side. She was worried about the pain that being on her side would cause her. She hadn't been able to lie on her side in a long time (due to her back pain).

They did come in and move her onto her side that night. They were very diligent about the care they gave so the bed ridden patients get moved regularly in order to avoid bed sores. I woke up each time they came into the room; however, I was usually able to fall asleep pretty easily after they left. I was relieved when they came to turn Sandy on her side since she didn't cry out in pain at all. She appeared very peaceful.

The Choice to Let Go

The choice to say goodbye.
The choice to let go.
The choice to know it's the end
of what we have always known.

The choice to say goodbye.
The choice to let go.
The choice to know the best is yet to be,
For those that are leaving the physical realm behind.

The choice to say goodbye.
The choice to let go.
The choice to be sad and glad
both at the same time.

The choice to say goodbye.
The choice to let go.
The choice to know it's not up to me,
What happens next is out of my hands.

The choice to say goodbye.
The choice to let go.
The choice to put your loved ones needs first,
To know that all will be alright once it's all said and done.

The choice to say goodbye.
The choice to let go.
The choice to know that in Truth:
We are all one and can never truly be parted.

The choice to say goodbye.
The choice to let go.
The choice to let them peacefully pass,
Into what in our humanness we cannot comprehend.

A JOYFUL SEASON OF SORROW

The choice to say goodbye.
The choice to let go.
The choice to let our human hearts cry
out in pain at a loss so great.

The choice to say goodbye.
The choice to let go.
The choice to let our Divine Nature
Bathe us in the Truth of our eternal connection.
The choice to say goodbye.
The choice to let go.
With love, strength, wisdom and understanding we have the faculties available to make:
The choice to say goodbye.
The choice to let go.

By Susan Smith

CHAPTER 12:

SILENT NIGHT

Sandy woke me up that morning. She was calling my name rather urgently, "Sue! Sue!" I got up quickly and rushed to her side. I was sure something was very wrong. "What's wrong?" I asked. "I'm lying on my side!" she said. "I'm lying on my side; I never thought I would be able to lie on my side again!" She was ecstatically happy. To think that she experienced that much joy simply because she was able to lie in a different position.

I was so happy to see her so happy. We talked for a few minutes. She was also very pleased that she was able to hold down the apple juice that she drank the night before. What a relief it was for her to be able to drink without the fear of throwing up afterwards. She told me know much she loved being at Peppi's House. She said that we can ask for whatever we want or need, and it will be brought to us at Peppi's House. She thought that being there was like being on a cruise ship. All they needed were cruise ship activities-like rollator races on the Lido deck. We talked about other fun activities they could have as well. I wonder if anyone else has likened an intake hospice unit to a cruise ship experience.

A JOYFUL SEASON OF SORROW

She told me how much we have to be grateful for. She was so sure she would never lie on her side again and there she was on her side. She was also looking forward to having Judy visit. After our talk, I took a few moments to use the restroom and get dressed for the day. When I came back into the room it was time for Sandy's spa treatment. I left the room while she received her spa treatment to make some calls. When I came back in the room Sandy looked so beautiful and peaceful. Her long hair was spread out on the pillow. It was so shiny. She was sleeping very deeply. It seemed that perhaps she had transitioned into a kind of unconscious state.

A couple of Sandy's friends came to visit her that morning. They drove down from Phoenix on Christmas Eve in order to see her. They were both teachers who had worked with Sandy at her last school. They told me how much Sandy had meant to them. She had been a role model to them. They also were thankful for how willing Sandy had been to share her gifts and talents with other teachers. Sandy was still "asleep" when they came. I was starting to realize at this point that she may never wake up. It became clear to me that it was possible that the last conversation we would have would be about how much we had to be grateful for.

I imagine Sandy's friends were disappointed that Sandy was not conscious and seemed unaware of their visit. I encouraged them to talk to her anyway. I know that she knew they were there and heard them even though she could not acknowledge them. While they were visiting, I went to the main hospital to visit Mom. Mom was doing much better and she was pretty aware. She was glad to hear that Sandy was getting such good treatment at Peppi's House and was happy to be there. Mom was happy to know that she was going to be released from the main hospital herself. Our hope was that she would be moved into Peppi's House that following day. After checking on Mom, I went back to check on Sandy. She was the same. Christine and Carrie were still visiting with her. I spent some time with the hospice social worker. She was very kind and listened attentively to our story. It was helpful to talk to her.

I returned to Sandy's room after Christine and Carrie left. As I sat down at Sandy's side, I knew that I would no longer be able to leave her alone anymore. I knew her time of transition was very near. I was hoping that Judy would make it on time. Judy had called just prior to boarding her plane. I had prepared her as best I could for Sandy's condition. I didn't want her to come in expecting Sandy to be conscious and find Sandy in what I thought was the last stage of her current physical life.

Fortunately, all was in Divine Order as I had made the arrangements with TMC hospice to move Mom to Peppi's House the next day already. I was able to concentrate my time and attention on Sandy during what I believed was to be her last hours with me in this physical realm. I also knew Judy would be there soon and I could check on Mom when she got there. It was interesting because none of the hospice nurses and/or doctor told me the end was near. Perhaps they just assumed I knew.

I was so happy to see Judy that afternoon. Sandy had said that she hoped that Judy would make it on time. I can't imagine how hard it must have been for Judy to see Sandy at this end stage. It had all happened so fast. The last time Judy had seen Sandy she had been strong and healthy. I told Judy she had come just in time as I knew I could no longer leave Sandy alone anymore.

Judy and I both planned to spend the night with Sandy. After a quick bite to eat from the Peppi's House pantry (amazingly I still had somewhat of an appetite). I left Judy by Sandy's side. I stopped in to check on Mom. I then went home to check on TK and to pack some things to take with me to Peppi's House. I remember I was just packing the beaded flowers I made for Sandy's Christmas present into my bag when I got the call. Judy told me that Sandy was gone. I was so glad that Judy had been there with her. I did not feel bad that I hadn't been by her side. At the exact moment the movie *Sound of Music* was showing on the television (we had the TV on to keep TK company while he was home alone). The Von Trap children were singing "So Long Goodbye" to the party guests in the background as Judy told me Sandy was gone. I believe that somehow Sandy was saying goodbye to me and TK through this song.

This song had always meant a lot to us. Sandy, Karen, and I used to sing and act out this song together.

I had told Sandy she should go when she was ready, and I had meant it. I told Judy I was on my way and then called our friend Diana to tell her and Joe the sad news. They were just packing up her car in order to come down to see Sandy. I was sorry that they didn't make it in time to see her. Joe was Sandy's now grown-up foster son. He was family to her and to me. At the same time, I recognized that Sandy probably had not wanted Joe's last memory of her to be on her deathbed. I was so relieved that Joe had called the night before and he had the chance to tell her how much he loved her, and she got to say what she needed to him. I know that call meant the world to her.

After I finished making this incredibly difficult call, I rushed back to Peppi's House. I remember crying very hard on my way there. Tears of sadness, tears of relief, tears of shock, tears that I knew would be the first of many I would shed to wash away my grief. Somehow, I made it there safely.

When I went into Sandy's room, I gave her beautiful face one last kiss. I thanked her amazing body for the wonderful service it had provided her beautiful soul all those years. Then I packed up the personal items we had in the room. Judy and I then sat on the couch. We waited for someone from Peppi's House to tell us what we needed to do next. Someone finally came in. We then realized they were giving us time and waiting for us in order to advise us about making the arrangements to take care of Sandy's body. We made the arrangements. It was hard to see them take her body away. I also knew that in many ways she was now freer than ever before. Her body wasn't her anymore.

 After we left Peppi's House we went to my mom's room at the main hospital. I thought I should tell her about Sandy, it seemed wrong that she didn't know what had happened. When we got there (Judy was with me) we explained the situation to the nurse. The nurse thought it would be better to wait until morning to tell Mom the news, especially since I would have to leave her to go home (I had a houseful of guests coming to visit). I am so glad she shared her opinion with me. I thought she was right. I couldn't tell my mom this news and then leave her. Since she was resting peacefully at the time, there was really no reason to tell her right away. I decided to come back in the morning to tell her about Sandy.

Shortly after I got home, we had a household full of guests. Judy, Diana, Joe, Leland, and Paula were all there to spend the night. It was nice to have them all there. These were all people who knew and loved Sandy. I think it would have been a very hard night if they had not been there. We talked and shared memories about Sandy. I shared about how peaceful she had been at the end. Everybody was sad and grieving in their own way. We were all still in the shock bubble as well. The situation seemed unreal to me, and I had seen the rapid deterioration of Sandy's health. I can't imagine how the others who hadn't been with her during this time were processing what happened. I remember making sure everyone had a place to sleep that night. Having these people who loved Sandy with me that night was extremely helpful. There are no magic words that help as we grieve. Simply the presence of others who loved our loved ones does wonders. I think it was around one am or so when we went to sleep that night.

It had been a memorable Christmas Eve. Somehow it seemed so fitting to me that Sandy died on a night when so many people in the world turn their attention to Peace on Earth. Sandy lived her life believing in contributing to the goal of having Peace on Earth. "Silent Night" was Sandy's favorite Christmas song (outside of Glen Campbell's "Gentle on My Mind"). I like to think that she could hear all the voices around the world singing this lovely song of peace as her soul transitioned from her body on that most holy of nights.

I did get a few hours' sleep that night. When I awoke it was dark out still. I went outside with TK. I looked up and saw the Big Dipper as clear as day. This was remarkable since I never recognize the constellations even when they are pointed out to me. I knew that somehow Sandy was making the stars shine brighter that morning as her way of letting me know what I knew in my heart, that all was well, and we can in truth never be parted.

Silent Night, Holy Night

Silent Night, Holy Night.
What a holy night,
To say goodbye to your beautiful body.

Silent Night, Holy Night.
I hope you heard
voices singing your favorite carol.
As your beautiful soul passed from this life we shared together.

Silent Night, Holy Night.
You believed in,
You worked for,
You embodied in all you did,
Peace and love throughout your life.

Silent Night, Holy Night.
The words of this song will now and forevermore be that much more holy to me.

As I remember the Christmas Eve
Your soul in human form said goodbye to me.

All is calm.
All is bright.
I know your soul
Is calm,
Is bright,
As you move onto the next stage of your journey.

By Susan Smith

CHAPTER 13:
CHRISTMAS DAY, PEPPI'S HOUSE PART II

My first thought when I woke up was that I wanted to be with my mom. I just needed to share my grief with her. While it was still dark out, Judy and I drove back to the hospital. I brought Best Bud (Sandy's snowman pillow present from TK) with me. Somehow with Judy's help I told Mom that Sandy had died the night before. Mom didn't have much to say when I told her. She did seem to understand at the time what we were saying. After we told her, she asked us to leave her alone for a while so she could rest. She had never asked to be left alone before, so I think she needed some private time to process this terrible news. We left her with Best Bud for a little while. I took Judy to the chapel, and we spent some quiet time there. I especially remember how much we both admired the beautiful manger they had in the chapel. I then showed Judy where Sandy's room had been in the hospital and my very own special shortcut back to Mom's room.

A JOYFUL SEASON OF SORROW

We had breakfast in the cafeteria that morning. Paula and Diana came to meet us. I remember thanking the people in the cafeteria for working on Christmas Day. I wanted them to know how much it meant to me and my family that they were there to serve us on that day. How strange it was to sit there and eat my breakfast with my friends knowing that my whole life had changed so dramatically just the night before.

Eventually I went back to sit with Mom. We got the good news that she was moving to Peppi's House that day. She was excited about the move and so was I. After she was transferred, all of my visiting friends came by to see Mom and me at Peppi's House. Mom's room was across the hall from where Sandy's had been. No one was in Sandy's room, so I showed it to Joe. He and Judy spent some time in there together. The rest of us spent time with Mom and hung out in the family area that was right next to Mom's room. There was a nice spread of food out for the holiday that we all enjoyed. I remember talking about Sandy and sharing good memories about her with them. What an odd Christmas Day it was for us all.

Eventually I encouraged Diana to take Leland and Joe back home to Phoenix. Paula also went back home, and I took Judy to our house to spend the night. I packed up a few things I needed and returned to Peppi's House in order to spend the night with Mom. I hadn't originally intended to spend the night. She asked me to, and I didn't see any reason why I couldn't be there for her. A part of me felt that Mom didn't have much time left. Plans were being made to arrange to have her come home. They seemed to think she had a few weeks to live at least. My instinct told me to treat the time we had together as if it was less than the doctor expected. With this thought in mind, I spent the next four nights at Peppi's house with my mom.

During that time, I made the arrangements for Sandy's remains. Judy kindly went with me to the mortuary. I was so glad I knew that Sandy wanted her body to be cremated. The mortuary director was very kind and guided me through the choices that were to be made. He didn't push me to purchase the most expensive item and/or try to talk me out any choices I made. He told me I was acting as an agent for Sandy. It helped me to think that I was an agent working on her behalf.

While Mom was in Peppi's House that week, she had many visitors. I had gotten the opportunity to contact her closest friends in Tucson and they had spread the word about her condition to those that I thought she would want to know. I did the same thing with her as I did with Sandy for her closest friends. I called and told them the sad news and then I gave the phone to Mom so she could talk to them herself. It was wonderful that so many people were able to come out to see her. It meant a great deal to her.

Her condition ebbed and waned, including her level of comprehension, throughout the week. Sometimes she seemed to be getting better and was her old self. Other times she was confused and didn't seem to know what was going on. Mom was happy to be in Peppi's House as compared to being in the hospital. The care was so much less intrusive. All the caregivers' concerns were about making her as comfortable as possible. She liked seeing the fountain that was on the patio outside her room. Mom had always loved fountains. One day a miniature horse, Sir Snickers, was brought into the room to visit (he was brought in through the patio door). She loved petting Sir Snickers. She was so pleased that people would be so kind to volunteer to bring him in to visit her and the other patients. It meant so much to her. She thanked the people for bringing him. Her words to me were, "Can you imagine people being so kind to me?" This is one of my favorite memories of her time at Peppi's House.

I was very thankful that they were able to keep her in Peppi's House while the arrangements were made to get her home. Arrangements were made for a hospital bed to be delivered to our home. I also had to arrange the furniture to make room for it in the living room. In addition, I needed to buy good sheets for it, etc.

This transition time was very helpful. I knew Mom wanted to come home. I wanted to make her wish come true. I also knew that she had fallen and hurt herself when I last cared for her at home. I had some fear that history might repeat itself. I understood that as nice as it would be for both of us to be home together, I would miss the support and expert care we were receiving at Peppi's House.

Once the arrangements were made and Mom knew the day she was coming home, she showed a marked improvement in her condition. Seeing her improvement at just hearing the news that she would be coming home soon gave me the added strength I needed in order to know we were doing the right thing by bringing her home. It also reminded me that I made this choice knowing with Understanding Faith that I will have all the resources, knowledge, ability, and strength I need in order to see that she received all the care she needed to be comfortable at home with me.

Although she was more content at Peppi's House, appreciated the good care and visit from Sir Snickers, Mom focused on coming home. I was also looking forward to getting home again as well. It would be good to be done with the drives back and forth to the hospital and home. I also knew that TK would be glad we were home. It would also be nice to be able to spend more time with Judy during her visit as she had planned to stay a couple of weeks. It was a tremendous support having her around. She helped out a great deal, it was good to have someone to share some of this experience with. I know she was also missing Sandy very much. It was good to be with someone who knew how I was feeling. I was looking forward to getting Mom home so we could all relax more and simply spend time being together.

Freedom, Freedom

Sometimes fear clouds my thoughts.
My adverse ego's warning system
Is screaming in my ear: Danger, Danger.
There is danger ahead:
Proceed with extreme caution!

My early detection warning system
is recognizing that there may be challenges ahead based on what has happened before.
My brain is doing data analysis using the input of all the sources of information that I have consulted throughout the years.
This data clearly indicates:
A code red warning is called for should I proceed on the course I am currently contemplating.

Now is the time to remember,
This code red warning
can be ignored.
It's based on factual evidence that is changing by the moment.

I remember I can spiritualize my ego.
Changing code red to code green.
By knowing that in Absolute Truth
I am Divinely Guided and protected always.
Truth is what I choose to consult as I decide the best course of action.
Facts I know are always changing and should be consulted warily.

My spiritualized ego now says:
Freedom, Freedom!
There is joy ahead!
Proceed with extreme enthusiasm!

By Susan Smith

CHAPTER 14:

FROM FEAR TO FREEDOM

We were very excited when the day arrived that Mom was coming home. We had the bed and we had everything ready for her. We put the bed in the living room right next to the couch that I would be sleeping on. Mom was very excited, all day she kept asking what will we be doing next? We had to wait until the afternoon for the transportation to arrive.

Judy went up to Sandy's house in Phoenix to get some of her things that day. She brought down some of Sandy's paperwork for me (I especially was looking for phone numbers and contact information for some of her friends). She drove up with my friends, Terry and Richard. She enjoyed the ride with them, she made another two friends.

Mom wanted to get up out of bed the morning she was leaving Peppi's House. This made me nervous. We called the nurse and she got her up with the help of a volunteer. This caused me some anxiety at first because I was not sure if I could get Mom up at home alone. I reassured myself that I will be able to do what I need to do when the time comes. She was so happy to be in the chair and I was glad that she had the comfort of sitting up and having her body in another position. I willed myself to let go of selfish concerns that I had about caring for her. I chose to simply focus all I could do to help her to be comfortable and strong. She also started to drink more as well. I have to confess that I was concerned for a moment that she had longer to live than expected. I feared what that meant for her and for me. She expressed that she was ready to go and perhaps she wasn't. I felt conflict and guilt about wanting this to be over quickly. I knew my fear stemmed from the difficulties that I had caring for her already and from her accident.

I found all these emotions really overwhelming. I knew I needed to feel my feelings and release the resultant thoughts that bringing her home was a bad idea because I was not up to the task of caring for her. At lunch time I took a break and went to a nearby park. I spent some time watching a father with his young child who was joyfully feeding the ducks. Watching them, I was reminded of all the times my mom was there for me and provided opportunities for me to feed the ducks and so much more. I felt the sadness come over me and I let myself cry out my sadness, my fear, my anger, my frustration, and my loneliness. With release and an understanding that these feelings would come and go, I was able to choose to be willing to forgive myself for these human thoughts and feelings. I released all to the Christ within that always knows the Truth. I affirmed that the best possible outcome would happen for her and that I would do all I could to help her. I was committed to caring for her as long as she needed me to and doing so out of love and not obligation. She had cared so selflessly for so many for so many years her whole life.

I helped Rhoda, one of the nurses' aides, with Mom's "spa treatment" that morning. I joked about how it seems that there is a special secret to the "spa treatment" between caregiver and patient. I was now being let in on the secret. I asked Rhoda if she wanted me to sign a waiver declaring that I would not reveal the secrets. As Rhoda was finishing up, I started to pack up our things to take with us. I put Best Bud in my bag. I explained to Rhoda I didn't want to forget anything this time as I lost the papers and books that I had forgotten in a drawer from Sandy's room. I realized this the next day and when I asked about them, I was told that everything must have been thrown out. She apologized and said usually they keep things like that. I said it was alright, that what I needed would come back to me in the end. Rhoda was sweet and said she would like to be like me. I appreciated her saying that. That morning I made some notes about the things I learned from Rhoda and the other hospice caregivers so could refer to them in order to take good care of Mom when I got her home. Everyone there was so kind and patient with me as they taught me what I needed to know in order to be the best caretaker I could be.

As I sat with Mom that afternoon waiting for the transportation person to come get her, I noticed that Mom was weak and seemed out of breath. It was painful to see her that way. Her condition changed so much every day. That morning when she woke up, she said she felt "wonderful." I was glad that she could still feel that way. I knew that I just needed to live moment to moment with her and not anticipate what was coming. Mom was thrilled when the driver came to pick her up to bring her home, I was excited as well.

I drove behind the van on the way back to the house. On the way home I had the radio playing. Both "Celebrate", and "I Hope You Dance" played on the radio during the drive. It seemed like the Universe was confirming that having Mom come home was the best choice for all of us. I especially appreciated hearing the song "I Hope You Dance" played since that was one of Sandy's favorite songs. As I drove, I couldn't help but remember driving behind the ambulance on Dec. 17th. How much had changed in such a short time.

Mom was so happy once she was settled into her bed in the house. She loved seeing the Christmas decorations (I had put up the decorations while I was caring for them both at home at the beginning of December), being greeted by TK and being out of the hospital altogether. The trip had tired her some. She was able to get some rest once we got home. All went well and I began to feel confident that everything was fine, and that I had nothing to fear about taking care of her by myself.

The next morning Mom mentioned that we needed to start getting her up so that she could get strong again. I told her I would be happy to help her get up to sit in a chair once Judy was home. I also explained to her that she was receiving hospice care. That she had rectal cancer and that she was not expected to get better. It was hard saying this to her and yet I felt like it was my job to fill in her memory. She thanked me for telling her this, and said she needed to know this. I remember she said then it is probably better if she goes sooner rather than later. All I said to this was that we would do all we could to make the most of the time she had remaining, however much time that would be.

The hospice nurse came to check on Mom that morning. Mom was very peaceful when the nurse came to visit. As usual Mom expressed appreciation and gratitude to the nurse for her help. I was also grateful to have this support, the nurse gave me a phone number to call in case I needed help. I was told I could call this number at any time day or night, and someone would be on call to answer my questions. She also gave me a package with special medicine I could administer should they tell me to give it to Mom to keep her comfortable. I was so grateful to have someone come to the house to care for Mom, especially considering how difficult it had been to get Mom to the doctor's visits we had earlier in the month. I also liked that I would not only be able to talk to someone about Mom, but they would be able to guide me in how to give her medicine should she need it.

That evening our friends Peggy and Bic came over and brought us a big meal. They brought chicken, salad, and pie! Judy and I loved the food. The pie was especially appreciated. It was so nice to have a hot delicious meal and not have to worry about doing the grocery shopping and cooking for ourselves.

The next couple days Mom rested a great deal. She had Best Bud with her, and she would often hug him to her. I asked her what she thought of Best Bud. She told me she liked having him. Having him made her feel less lonely when she was alone. At one point she asked about where Sandy was. Judy and I explained that Sandy was in a better place. Then Mom remembered that Sandy had died.

A JOYFUL SEASON OF SORROW

She didn't talk too much. I could tell she was happy to be at home. She had wanted to get up the first day to sit in a chair. I asked her to wait for Judy to come home so she could help us. By the time Judy got home Mom didn't want to get up anymore. After that she never asked to get up. She really wasn't drinking much, and she wasn't eating at all. It wasn't difficult to care for her. She had a catheter, so I didn't have to worry about bed pans, etc. I gave her the daily spa treatments, gave her water to sip on, keep her lips moist with Vaseline, shifted her bed position (I was very proud I learned how to do this-I was even able to change the bed sheets with her in the bed!), and made sure she had fresh gowns every day. Mostly I was simply there for her.

We talked a little. I told her that we had a bunch of leaves in the back yard that needed to be picked up. She had always found the chore of picking up the leaves a major inconvenience. She totally surprised me this time when I told her about the leaves, and she said with a smile that she wanted to go walk in the leaves, that she had always loved walking in the leaves. This was a good reminder to me about treasuring every moment we have as we never know when it will be a last opportunity in this lifetime for something as simple and beautiful as walking in the leaves.

Judy and I played cards, ate pie (chocolate pecan with some liquor flavoring), and watched the Roswell TV show DVDs. We had fun watching the show, I enjoyed sharing one of Sandy and I's favorite shows with her. We kept the volume down so as to not disturb Mom. Judy wore the TV ears and I read the subtitles.

Joy Is Absolute

Joy is Absolute.
Joy is Truth.
Joy is under all.
Joy is best shared.
Joy is all around.
Sadness is relative.
Joy is a choice.

Sadness is relative.
Sadness is circumstance based.
Sadness is transitory.
Sadness can be transmuted.
Joy is a choice.

When faced fearlessly,
When shared fully,
When not hidden from view in silence,
When brought into the light of Truth,
Sadness is transmuted.
Joy is a choice.

Sadness is relative.
Sadness is circumstance based.
Sadness is transitory.

Sadness can be transmuted when tears are shed.
Tears are the elixir,
Changing sadness to joy.
Like the alchemist shaped metal into gold.
Sadness and joy can coexist.
As to feel sadness means
A source of joy now appears to be gone
From one's life.

A JOYFUL SEASON OF SORROW

In Truth we know
Nothing beautiful can ever be gone.
Nothing beautiful truly can leave.
Love never leaves.
The physical vehicle may be gone.
The spirit may be separated from the being.
But the Love goes on and on.
We are eternal always.
We leave our love with all when we
Let go of this physical life.
Love never leaves.
Love permeates all.
Love couldn't be seen before or after death.
Love is ours to cherish always.

By Susan Smith

CHAPTER 15:

NEW YEAR'S

On New Year's Eve morning, Mom and I had a nice conversation about the Christmas decorations. She was so glad that the house was decorated. She loved looking at the decorations. She especially loved the mitten lights that she had bought from a friend the previous summer. It was funny because she complained one time about being "ripped off" because they didn't work. We explained to her they weren't plugged in. Of course, I plugged them in, and she saw that they were indeed working after all. She also expressed that she was happy that we had Barry come over to help put up the lights outside. She thought our house looked beautiful. I mentioned that we will have to call him back soon to help take down the decorations. She asked me to please wait a few days. This was so uncharacteristic of her. She always wanted to get the decorations down once New Year's Day rolled around. Of course, I told her we would take the decorations down when she was ready to have them down.

At some point that day she asked about when the others were coming. I asked her who she was referring to and she said my sisters, Sandy and Karen. I explained that they had died, and she would be seeing them when she passed.

She understood and was happy that she would be seeing them soon. This was interesting because she had never expressed a belief in any type of afterlife and yet she seemed to completely accept this as fact when I said this to her. She also told me that she sees me even when her eyes are closed. I said I was always with her and that she would see me after she was gone as well, just like I would see and know she was with me.

That morning her good friend Evaleen came to visit. Mom was in and out of the conversation during her visit. Judy and Evaleen shared stories while Mom mostly listened. I took the opportunity at that time to visit the neighbors to give them updates. The rest of the day Mom barely talked and rested peacefully.

On New Year's Eve night, Mom was very restless. I made several calls to the on-call hospice nurse to ask for guidance about how to help Mom. She even gave me her cell phone number so I could more easily get in touch with her. The nurse was very helpful and kind. Mom was restless and seemed to be in pain. I gave her some pain medicine and managed to get her settled and more comfortable. Eventually I laid down on couch in order to get some sleep. I realized at that point that Mom was simply going through part of the dying process and I had done all I could to help her. I know I didn't sleep much as I wanted to be sure to hear her should she need my help in any way. I remember hearing people celebrating the coming of the New Year. At that time, I checked on Mom, and she was at last resting peacefully. She was resting so peacefully that I chose not to shift her in the bed as I had been doing on the previous nights. I didn't want to disturb her.

On the first day of the New Year, I woke up and I saw that Mom was resting comfortably. She seemed peaceful except for her breathing which was labored. There was also a rattling sound when she breathed. She had taken off her gown and covers in the night when she had been restless.

I really had wanted to cover her up the night before as it was cold in the house, and she looked so vulnerable uncovered. I let her be because I knew it had been her choice to uncover herself and she would just push down the covers again and take off the gown again if I covered her up. I was glad she was so much more peaceful that morning. I got a fresh gown and pulled up the covers (typically she was always really cold). She needed to be pulled up on the bed, but I was afraid to disturb her, so I left her as she was.

Later on in the morning I called Roseann (the on-call nurse) to ask about pain medication. During the night the on-call nurse had me give some medicine to Mom when she was expressing discomfort. Since Mom was resting peacefully in the morning Roseann and I agreed that I did not need to give Mom any more medicine unless she woke up and needed it. Since she had a difficult night and seemed to have transitioned to a new stage Roseann arranged to have one of the other on call nurses, Oak, come out to check on Mom.

Oak arrived later in the morning; it was a relief to have her there. She was so gentle and kind in the care she gave to Mom, and in her support to me and Judy. She helped me adjust Mom in the bed. I explained I had been afraid to move her and thus disturb her. She also cleared out the foam that was coming out of Mom's mouth. She showed me how to take care of that myself. She assured me that Mom was peaceful at this point and that she didn't need pain medicine. She also told me what to look for in case Mom might need more pain medicine later (which she never did). I asked her if she thought Mom would be aware and talking again. She said she didn't think so. Her visit was extremely helpful, she eased my concerns about whether or not I was doing what I could to make Mom as comfortable as possible. I again felt confident in the choice I made to bring Mom home.

That afternoon I left Judy at home with Mom, and I went to pick up some groceries for us. It was difficult for me as I kept seeing things I would have bought for Sandy or Mom. I realized how hard even the most everyday chores were going to be for me in the near future.

The rest of the day Judy and I played cards and continued our Roswell marathon. Mom never woke up. I did what I could to keep her as comfortable as possible. She seemed to be in a kind of semi-conscious state. That night I gave Mom a kiss goodnight at 9:00 pm. I then fell asleep on the couch. At 10:00 pm I woke up and looked over at Mom. I realized that her labored breathing had come to an end. I went to check on her and realized that Mom had passed away. I was so glad that it had been a peaceful end for her. It had always been her wish to die in her sleep in her bed at home. I woke up Judy and told her I thought Mom was gone. She came out and confirmed that indeed Mom's soul had departed. We then made the necessary arrangements to care for Mom's body.

New Year

It's a New Year
I hear the people cheer.
Happy New Year! They are all screaming!

It's good to hear the celebrations.
It's good to know life continues on
Even as we are involved in our own drama.

I knew you wouldn't be here long as this New Year was ushered in.
I could tell your restlessness had been a part of your soul preparing to move on.
I'm so glad I was by your side that New Year's morning.
There was no place I'd rather be.
 I'm glad you seemed at peace at last as we brought in the year 2012.

I wished the world a good cheer when I awoke and heard the shouting.
I turned aside then and went back to sleep.
I knew I had to be ready for whatever the
The New Year would bring in the morning.

We didn't converse with one another on that New Year's Day.
You seemed to be half here half gone.
I didn't want to get in your way,
As I could tell you were getting ready to move on.

I'm glad you passed as you wanted,
Peacefully in your sleep.
How very strange it was to know the New Year would pass without you in it.

I knew you knew I was alright.
That I could deal with you leaving.
I felt your love then and now it means so much to me.

A JOYFUL SEASON OF SORROW

To flip the calendar that year was to flip onto the new adventure, that now awaited me, as I embarked on a living a life without your physical presence.

By Susan Smith

The Golden Thread of Love

The golden thread of love
Is sewing my heart back together.
The golden thread of love
Will make all things right again.

The golden thread of love
Is stronger than any other power.
The golden thread of love
Will make me whole again.

The golden thread of love
Is available always to those who call for it.
The golden thread of love
Is in each ray of sunshine.
The golden thread of love
Is in each smiling face I encounter.
The golden thread of love
Is in each opportunity I have to practice forgiveness.
The golden thread of love
Connects me eternally to all.

The golden thread of love
Helps my heart beat stronger than ever,
As I move forward boldly in this new life I am creating.
The golden thread of love
Holds the warm memories in my heart.
Allowing me to look forward to today and the tomorrows that lay before me with joy happiness and peace.
The golden thread of love
Mends my heart so that it is wide open to all I meet.

By Susan Smith

A JOYFUL SEASON OF SORROW

I transcribed a couple of the prayers I wrote in the Peppi's House prayer journal when I went back there. The first one I wrote on Christmas Day after Sandy had died. The second one I wrote when we were preparing to bring Mom home from Peppi's House.

Dear Oneness, (God, Spirit, Divine Principle)

Guide my sister as she transitions from this life to her new life. Let her know how loved she was and how much she will be missed. Now it is the time for her to be peaceful and this is all I want for her.

Help me have the strength to let her go, to feel both the joy in this transition as she takes on her new spiritual journey, and the sadness of losing her in this life that we have shared together for so many years. I rest in the assurance that although there is no longer a physical body for me to touch and talk to in this physical world, we are as connected on the deepest and truest level as we ever were. We are made of love. Our love connection is eternal both before her passing and now as well. I rest in the assurance as well that as she leaves this physical world behind and those of us who loved her here, she has now been greeted with joy and celebration by those that we lost in the past that were waiting to greet her with love that never can end.

So, I release to you with joy of the revelation and with sadness for the loss of her physical presence a willingness to feel what I need to feel, to do what needs to be done to focus on what needs to be focused on so I can move and heal my seemingly broken heart. Amen

Dear God,

I release to you any expectation I have about what the future might bring. I know that I don't need to know when the pain will end when my heart will mend. [I was quoting Daniel Nahmod in my prayer here]

Today I set the intention to release any worry or concern about what I need to do for my mother. I rely on the Christ within, the still silent voice to guide me. I have faith that I will have invisible aid at all times. Whenever I feel a need for it.

I pray that my mom be comfortable. That she is able to do the work she needs to do in order to pass from this life to the next part of her journey. I know that within her, the truth resides that although I will be really sad to lose her that we will always be connected, and her physical death will not change this. I know that Divine Love surrounds her and will let her know that I will be fine and that it is alright for her to leave me now physically as this is her time to go.

We are one. We are always one. I focus on the now gently reviving happy memories and keeping my concerns about a changed future to a minimum. Thanks for all. Amen,

A JOYFUL SEASON OF SORROW

Sandy wrote letters one night when she was in the hospital. Here are transcriptions of two of them:

Transcription of Sandy's letter to her friends:

To my friends,

I have thought about what one can do at a time like this. If you would like to do something, please celebrate with friends as you would any other change in your life. If that is to have a party go for it. If you would like to do one more thing, possibly find a way to help someone who won't expect it and may never know you did it-One time I went to a restaurant with a friend and ate a $12 meal. We left a $20 tip and walked away. I'll be smiling and hopefully so will you. Life is a gift and I have enjoyed every moment of mine. I wish you the same.

Sandy

Transcription of Sandy's letter to me:

Sue,

I love you so much. Thank you for being an amazing sister, person, and friend. I could not have gotten through this and so many things, without your friendship and love. I admire you so much. Your true belief in others that has you approaching them with such kindness. The way you helped my neighbor while most walked by. The way you helped Helen get up to sing with the choir.

I now hope to be an added force to your life to spread goodness. If you see a little burst of wind, it is me taking your goodness, kindness, and belief further along.

I'll love you always and will be with you in your traveling vacation thinged [I'm not sure what this word is]-

You can't ever lose what you had-I am glad I _have_ you.

Sandy

Transcript of Sandy's Obituary:

Smith, Sandra L. (Sandy)

peacefully passed away on December 24, 2011. She was preceded in death by her father Fred Smith and her sister Karen Armenta. Her mother Jerry Smith died shortly after her on January 1, 2012. She is survived by her sister Susan Smith and her foster son Joseph Madrigal. Sandy was a passionate, talented, and dedicated educator who touched and enhanced countless lives. Rocket launches, egg drop contests, solar cooker creations, and/or high interest reading groups were a few activities she did to engage her students (whom she always believed in 100%) in learning. Many were fortunate throughout her life to call her teacher, principal, collaborator, and friend throughout Arizona, New Mexico and Cairo, Egypt. Her positive attitude, kindness, and compassion (she always believed she could make the world a better place) will be missed by her family, friends and students. In lieu of flowers Sandy asked that people perform a random act of kindness to a stranger in memory of her. [The rest was details about her celebration of life party]

A JOYFUL SEASON OF SORROW

Transcript of Mom's Obituary:

Smith, Geraldine M. (Jerry)

peacefully passed away on Sunday, January 1, 2012. Jerry was proceeded in death by her husband, Fred and her two daughters, Sandy Smith and Karen Armenta. She is survived by her daughter, Susan Smith. Jerry will be missed by her family and the many friends she touched in her generous, adventurous, and wonderful life. Jerry was a woman who made the most of her 82 years of life. Her daughter, lifelong friends, exercise buddies, card playing partners and neighbors will all remember the great times they had with her. [The rest was details about her celebration of life party and donation request in lieu of flowers]

CHAPTER 16:
WIDE OPEN HEART AND THE UNITY 5 PRINCIPLES

Thus, the most unusual and difficult holiday season of my life ended that New Year's Day. From Thanksgiving Day to New Year's Day, we had all been on one extraordinary roller coaster ride. On Thanksgiving Day, I could never have imagined that both Mom and Sandy would have departed this world come the New Year. For the next several weeks after Mom died, I was busy making arrangements for celebration parties in memory of each of them. I had a party at Mom's house to celebrate her life for her friends. I had a party at Sandy's house to celebrate her life in Phoenix. I contacted many of the people that we just did not have time to contact before that loved and valued Sandy. I was supported so much by many friends who went above and beyond to be there for me.

Although there is no doubt I had some very difficult moments, I sometimes ask myself how I got through all this as well as I did. Certainly, the strength and courage that both Mom and Sandy had, and how they conducted themselves during these weeks of grave illness as well as how they each went through the dying process, were a tremendous source of strength and courage for me. I also know that by using my spiritual tools and the foundation of my faith, I was able to take what were truly unimaginable circumstances and choose what my experience of those circumstances would be. I believe because of the time I have invested in study, the teachers I have had and my willing heart to develop my spiritual practice, I can now look back on this time without regret and with deep gratitude, that I could be there with my mom and sister during this deeply spiritual time in their lives.

As a student of Unity, my spiritual practice has been deeply grounded in what we refer to as the Five Basic Principles. These principles express the core beliefs of Unity. They are not necessarily a doctrine, they can be interpreted in different ways, and they are a generally accepted way of expressing the core beliefs of Unity. Here are the five principles and an accounting of how my understanding of these principles (which is unique to me and ever changing as I grow and evolve) and how they intertwine within each other, helped me shape these unimaginable circumstances into an experience of my own choosing.

Principle 1: God Is: There is One Power, One Presence.

In Unity we believe there is One Power, One Presence, which we often call God. Unity is also very accepting and open to people calling this power by whatever name that serves them best. This One Power is all presence, all power, and knowledge in expression. When we refer to that which we call God we are not referencing a deity that has human characteristics that controls the fate of humans. In Unity that which we call God is principle, it is unchanging, and it is always present whether we recognize it or not.

It was my foundational understanding faith of this principle that helped me when I was struggling with dealing with the challenges put before me. When I felt frustrated, confused, deeply saddened, or angered by what was happening I reminded myself that that which we call God stands under all and that which we call God is ever present and good without opposite. Knowing I was always on firm ground no matter what was happening helped keep me centered. By being centered I was able to go forward one step at a time to do what was mine to do.

Sometimes the step before me was really hard to take, and there were times when Mom and Sandy were so sick, that it seemed that everything that was happening was as far removed from Good without Opposite as possible. It was especially frustrating when we were not getting answers to our questions about why they both were so ill. It was so hard because I knew they were both suffering so much and there was so little I could do to help them. When I began to feel frustrated by this, I would remind myself that Good is always present and true divine order is always at work in our lives. I knew that we had to do what was ours to do and wait in the fullness of time for divine wholeness (an understanding of the eternal perfect divine being each of us is) to be restored to both of them. Reminding myself that Good without Opposite (how I like to refer to that which we call God) and divine order was in place helped me to shift from fear to faith. This was probably one of the most challenging things I had to do during this whole series of events.

Because I chose to know that good was present even when things got so difficult, I believe I was able to see Good without Opposite and divine order operating in our lives then and am able to reflect upon this even more now in hindsight. For instance, I never ever would have wanted my mother to suffer as she did when she fell the night I took Sandy to the hospital. I never would have wanted to come home to find out that my worst fear had happened and that Mom had gotten up, fallen, and hurt herself when I left her alone. Now I see that it was a blessing in disguise to have Mom in the hospital when Sandy was there. Having her there made it possible for me to spend more time with Sandy. Having her there meant they were finally able to identify what was wrong with her. Having her there meant that she and Sandy got to visit and say goodbye, and they had the closure they needed. Having her there meant I was no longer helplessly watching as she suffered. Having her there meant

A JOYFUL SEASON OF SORROW

I had partners in her care that I could talk to and rely on. Having her in the hospital, as terrible as the regrettable circumstances around her admission were, was a blessing in disguise. I know that as strange as it seems, Good was present and divine order was in place that led to her admission to the hospital that dark December night.

Good was also in evidence to me when Mom's condition warranted her admission to a ward where she received extra care and attention. Because of this I was able to comfortably leave her for longer periods knowing she was getting the very best care possible. The placement of her room and Sandy's was also very fortuitous. TMC is a very big one-story hospital. Sandy and Mom were in two separate wards and there was a shortcut between their two rooms. I could literally take a 5-minute walk to go from one room to the other even though they were in different wards of the hospital.

Upon reflection after everything that has happened, I even realized that having them both sick at the same time as they were and dying within 8 days of each other was a blessing in disguise as well. If one or the other had gotten sick a month, two, or six after the other had died; I think it would have been that much harder on us. I think if that had happened, we would have thought: "Here we go again!" Of course, I would have liked to have had more time with both of them and yet since this was not to be even at the time, I could see the blessing in the timing of these circumstances we found ourselves in. A part of me thinks that Mom's intuition knew that she was about to lose another child and she just couldn't go through that again. Mom's health had been in decline for the past year, and I do not think it was a coincidence that it took a big decline at the same time as Sandy's did. There is no way to know why things happened as they did or what would have happened had things been different. I know that I believe that the way things happened was a blessing in disguise.

Good was present and order was operational even if it didn't seem like it at the time. Grounding my faith in this principle and thus recognizing that as it's been said, "There is not a spot where God is not," allowed me to often see and recognize all the good present and the order amidst these difficult times. Being able to recognize the good and order present allowed me to let go and know that we are indeed supported even when everything seemed to be going terribly wrong and I wasn't able to recognize anything positive about the circumstances that we found ourselves in. Understanding faith sometimes requires us to close our eyes to the outer temporal material conditions to see all the good always available to us to see (love, peace, wisdom, strength, order).

Principle 2: I Am: I am a divine human and am connected to everyone and everything.

This second principle affirms my understanding that each of us is an expression of Spirit. This also means we are all connected to one another and connected to all the wisdom we need when we need it. This means that I understand that we are one. I am you and you are me. This principle also assures me that we are each timeless eternal beings that cannot ever be separated from each other, even as we our loved ones go through the process, we call death.

Having an understanding faith in our connection to one another helped me to let go of my human adverse ego's need to know what was happening, what was mine to do, and what the future would look like. I understood and had faith that by listening to divine guidance (also called intuition) I would ascertain the wisdom I needed in order to be where I needed to be when I needed to be there and to do what I needed to do in order to support my mom and sister. Since we are all connected in ways inexplicable to the temporal human me, I knew that I needed to relax and let Spirit, of which I am an expression, guide me. Also, by understanding my connection to all, and that everyone is an expression of the divine, I was willing to have faith that the people we met along the strange path we were on would care for, guide, and direct us to the highest and best outcome possible for all of us.

The burden of making decisions, speaking the words I needed to say, and taking the actions that were mine to do was eased greatly by my understanding of the fact that I, as an expression of Spirit, am divinely guided. When I remembered to let go and know that I have the inner wisdom and connection to all the wisdom I needed at the moment, I moved forward usually with assurance and peace, knowing that I would always know the right next step to take. I knew the big picture was too much for me to take in, but I also knew that I would always know what was mine to do at that moment in time as I am connected to all and that I am a conduit of the wisdom of the ages. As it's been said, "All the answers are inside of me." Letting go of my personal need to know, and letting my inner divine nature guide me served me in so many ways during this time. It wasn't always easy to do this and sometimes I would regret something I said or did, but I always knew that each moment was fresh and new, and I had the potential to do the best next thing always.

My understanding of the second Unity principle also eased my pain and grief as my loved ones went through the dying process, and eventually moved on to their next stage of being. As hard as it was to know that our time to say goodbye to one another was coming much sooner than expected, I also always knew that love never dies and our connection was eternal. I knew that the end of their physical life was really a stage of transitioning into something new for both of them.

Recognizing and remembering the wholeness and inherent divinity within myself, Mom and Sandy and everyone else who traveled this path with us, gave me the confidence to face and make with relative ease, seemingly impossible choices about where to be, what to say and how to help. I knew that it was "not I but the Christ inside" that knew the way forward. Facing circumstances that were beyond my personal ability to process, I realize now that I probably have never surrendered more fully to this principle and understanding before or since. I truly as, it's been said, "Let go and let God." Knowing Mom and Sandy's nature was whole and divine (even though they were experiencing so much pain and suffering) and that our connection could not ever be broken, was extremely comforting and was foundational in allowing me to be fully present and to say goodbye to them as this part of the journey we shared together was coming to an end.

Principle 3: I Think: I create my experiences by what I think, feel, and believe.

Our third Unity principle is the premise behind the Law of Mind action. The premise is that "thoughts held in mind tend to manifest after their own kind." We understand that our consciousness-the thoughts we have, the stories we tell ourselves, and the words we share about our thoughts, shape our experience of the circumstances that happen in our lives. The thoughts we give time and attention to tend to produce like-minded thoughts. As we have like-minded thoughts, we are going to recognize and resonate with more things in our circumstances that align with the way we are thinking.

Looking back at these events I recognize that we utilized this principle as best we could at the time with the situation we were facing. I was not able to deny the facts of both Mom and Sandy's declining health. It wouldn't have been helpful if I could have, as Unity does not teach us to deny facts. I saw consistent evidence that neither of their physical bodies were functioning as they should. I found it difficult to affirm either of their physical wholeness since the evidence before me was of their pain and suffering. Although I couldn't deny the facts of the evidence of their declining health and the challenges that they were facing I could deny that their physical condition determined their wellbeing. I was able to affirm all the spiritual attributes that were always true about each of us no matter what circumstances we are facing. I affirmed their strength, wisdom, dominion, imagination, etc. I affirmed that they were divine eternal beings now and always.

Facing the facts (and not letting them have the last word as I have been taught) I also remained as positive about the possibility for improvement of their conditions as I could possibly have been. Until each of them was diagnosed and I saw the pattern of their passing emerging, I always held out hope that we would find out what was wrong with each of them, and they would receive treatment that would alleviate their suffering and restore their physical health.

A JOYFUL SEASON OF SORROW

When that hope was gone and in the dark moments of despair, I allowed myself to be willing to know that higher Truth was operating, despite appearances to the contrary. I also relied on my spiritual community and our friends to hold this high watch for us during this time. Being in a community that can support and know the higher absolute truth, was invaluable to me since the evidence of their challenges were a daily reality for me and it was difficult for me to affirm the Truth that divine perfection was expressing at the point of those challenges.

One thing I did my best to avoid or at least to recognize and let go of was indulging consciously in metaphysical guilt and malpractice. Blaming oneself for the circumstance of one's life and expecting one's ability by the "simple" act of changing your thinking to improve upon those circumstances is called metaphysical malpractice or sometimes metaphysical guilt. Malpractice is when we blame someone's challenges on the quality of their thinking and perhaps "lack of faith." It is called guilt if we do this to ourselves. This is such a destructive and unhelpful practice that I don't even like writing about it. It is one of the shadow sides of New Thought and the Unity belief systems and it's important to recognize it for what it is. It is based on a misplaced understanding of the law of mind action. This is also a prevalent culture issue we face here in the United States. We talk about people who are battling and/or are survivors of cancers as fighters who are strong minded and willful. People who have the right attitude and "can beat this thing" are regarded highly and lauded for their ability to stay strong and think positive no matter what. While this kind of talk can be motivational, at the same time it can be harmful when people, due to their own inner knowing and understanding of their body, come to accept their prognosis and others judge them harshly or question why "they are giving up." When we refer to shaping the experiences of our lives through our thoughts, we are not referring to the transient state of the material circumstances of which everyone is subject to. We are talking about how we shape the experience of our circumstance based on the thoughts we focus on and harmonize with regardless of whether the outer conditions in which we find ourselves would be considered more or less favorable to ourselves.

Knowing about Charles and Myrtle Fillmore's (Unity co-founders) healing stories and other Unity teachers' stories of physical healing, it would have been easy for me to fall victim to a form of metaphysical malpractice and guilt during these days in which Mom and Sandy were both so gravely ill. I can't imagine myself ever holding them accountable in any way for their circumstances but blaming myself is another matter. Even today as I write this, there is a small portion of my thought process which silently whispers to me, as it did at the time, that if I only had had more faith and thought right, I could have saved them. If only I had prayed more regularly and truly believed in the restoration of their physical wholeness, things would have turned out differently. If I only I had been able to affirm with all my faith that in Truth they were complete, perfect, and whole no matter what the facts to the contrary appeared to be, I would have been able to do more for them. If only I had been stronger in my mind, smarter in my thinking and had more faith, then they have may not have both died. When these thoughts enter into my mind now or back then I do/did my best not to entertain them as they are all forms of Metaphysical guilt. Thoughts come and go and when guilty thoughts of how my thinking may be manifesting something undesirable or not manifesting a desirable result, I gently deny their power over me.

I remember when I was caring for Sandy at home, she knew a little about the Unity principles and about the Fillmore's healing stores, she expressed her own feelings of failure and guilt in regard to how her thoughts brought about her illness. She told me that she thought the people who started Unity probably never would have found themselves in this kind of situation. It was easy for me to assure her that she should not feel guilty about how her own thinking may have caused her illness. In Unity we recognize that circumstances come and go in our lives. Charles and Myrtle Fillmore eventually both did end up with illnesses that ended their lives. They also had a son who died when he was young adult. They had demonstrated healing and wholeness and faced challenging circumstances. I encouraged Sandy to let go of these feelings of guilt as they were neither helpful nor warranted.

For me, the law of mind action is a helpful tool. That means we aren't to blame ourselves or the thoughts we hold/held for the circumstances we find ourselves in. We live in collective consciousness and factual events of our lives are products of this consciousness. Circumstances in our lives come and go. The practical use of the law of mind action and the practice of affirmative prayer are helpful, useful tools and are not to be used in any way to punish ourselves, or to feel inadequacy when facing difficult life conditions. Our tools are here to help us. They are not intended to make us feel bad about what we thought that brought about this event and/or why we can't think right in order to make the situation better.

One of the helpful ways I used the law of mind action was to be very conscious about how I was using my power/ability of love during these times of challenge. Love is one of our or inherent abilities (or powers). Love is the ability to desire. Love is the power that we use to harmonize and "attract" things to ourselves. It is the power behind what is called the power of attraction (a phrase I am personally not fond of as it simplifies and at the same time complicates a deeply spiritual practice). Simply put, whatever we focus our attention and thoughts on is what we love at the time. Love is neutral. If we are complaining about something in a non-constructive manner (meaning we are just sharing our frustration and not taking actions or providing fuel to take action to improve the situation), we are truly loving what we are complaining about and harmonizing and recognizing other things we have to complain about. If we focus our time, words, and thoughts on the positive aspects of the circumstances before us we are harmonizing with what we have to be grateful and appreciative of. When we become conscious of the choice before us, we can exercise the option to choose what we tune ourselves to and thus harmonize with. So, we can love and harmonize with that which we do not want to have in our lives due to the time and attention we put on those very things. The opposite is true as well. The more we harmonize (focus our time, words, and attention) with the positive, the more positive we will recognize and experience. This is the basis of the Law of Attraction; however, I believe a better way to describe the power of love in operation is to visualize oneself tuning a radio dial into the station that we desire to resonate with and listen to. This is a metaphor I've heard before and I have always found it helpful.

Throughout the time I was supporting Mom and Sandy I consciously focused my thoughts as much as possible on what I wanted to harmonize with. I knew that my faculty of love was at work and that it was neutral. I knew, therefore, that if I was to focus my thoughts and words on fear and anger I would have more to be fearful and angry about. I consciously acted from my power of love. When I found myself holding onto thoughts that were not productive and in ways, I did not want to increase, I used the mind action spiritual tools of positive music, positive imagining, and humor as well as prayer, gratitude, and denials, and affirmations, to gently shift to the positive that I knew was always present no matter what was happening.

One of the main tools that helped me to shift my thinking during this time from fear to faith was the power of positive music. Music has always been a channel for me in how I interpret and interact with the world and by being selective about my music I could choose what thought patterns or things I wanted to increase in my consciousness. Growing up we watched many musicals and listened to the top 40 radio stations. When we lived together Sandy and I used to make up songs about what was going on. TK even had his own theme song! I have often thought how great life would be if it was truly a musical.

When I learned about the law of mind action, I realized that many of the songs I enjoyed had either meaningless or negative lyrics. I knew that the lyrics I had imbedded in my conscious were a powerful creative force. I recognized that I needed to be more conscious about the choices of music that I listen to and allowed to become part of my internalized thought process. I began to develop a collection of new positive/new thought music. My playlists are now full of songs from Daniel Nahmod, Karen Druker, Faith Rivera, Terri

Wilder, Eddie Watkins Jr. (to name a few). These are some of the artists and music we listen to during services and in classes at Unity services. I have also had the privilege of seeing many of these artists in concert. Often the words of these positive songs, so full of Spirit, full of truth and full of love, arose in my consciousness when the sadness, pain and fear were threatening to overwhelm me.

Two of the songs that I remember that came to mind frequently during this time to assist my shift in thinking were Daniel Nahmod (Nahmod 2022) songs. The one song is titled, "I Don't Need to Know." The lyrics to this song came to my mind many times when I just didn't know what to do, how to do it, and/or how to get through it. Remembering the words to this song affirmed the truth that I AM always on firm ground and that God (Truth, Spirit) stands under all. These lyrics supported me when I felt immobilized by fear and uncertainty. Hearing these words repeat, within my mind, the message that I can let go of my personal need to control and know that which we call God, is ever present in the midst of all circumstances. Bringing these lyrics to mind helped me when I felt a need to transition from fear to faith. The lyrics to this song also supported me when I found myself almost overwhelmed with the pain and sadness due to the losses that I was experiencing. The truth and this wisdom of these lyrics was imbedded in my consciousness by the time these events occurred, due to that fact I was able to remember them when I needed them most. Bringing these words to mind strengthened me tremendously.

I also found the lyrics to the Daniel Nahmod song, "Love Is My Decision," coming to mind frequently during this time. Simply repeating the title to this song reminds me that I can always choose love. Having the lyrics to this song playing in my head were the guidepost I used to remind myself I have the power to choose love and it will always be available to me. The lyrics of this song served to remind me that I have the power of dominion over my thoughts. I get to choose to love and what I love in any moment. With love for my family, our loved ones, my spiritual community, and our caregivers as the foundation of my thoughts I knew that no matter what was happening everything would be alright. With "Love as My Decision" I would always know what was next to do and the road of truth would be laid clear before me.

During this time, I affirmed even more firmly the knowledge that positive music is a mighty tool in the practice of positive mind action. Being musically minded, I am so thankful for every single artist that has taken the time and effort to share their creative gifts and talents with the world. As a person who hears life as a musical, having positive music imbedded in my consciousness is a constant source of support, joy and strength in my efforts to be the best I can be.

Another law of mind action tool I used to shape these circumstances was consciously using my power of imagination. I used to have a severe habit of worrying and stress. This habit was particularly strong since I do have a powerful imagination. I was exceptional at imagining all the worst-case scenarios of what could happen in my life. Twenty years ago, while taking a Dale Carnegie course and reading his book, *How to Stop Worrying and Start Living*, I learned and began applying a lot of helpful tools to beat the worrying habit. One of the habits I had to break was imagining the worst-case outcomes for whatever I was worrying about at the time. I pretty much kicked this habit for good or at least got a very good handle on it. I learned to lock out all the stories I created in my head about what could happen in the future. When I learned of the positive power of the imagination through my Unity coursework, I was slightly afraid of unlocking the door to what had once been a destructive power: my imagination. Through practice I have learned how to use my imagination as a creative force for good in my life.

For instance, I used my imagination to visualize Mom coming home from Peppi's House. I gently let go of the images I had of her falling or of my not being able to care for in the way she deserved. Instead, I saw her happy and comfortable in her hospital bed in the living room. I visualized myself caring for her and being able to see to her needs. I saw TK, happy to have us home and sharing his joy with us that he wasn't home alone anymore. I pictured myself easily getting any help I needed. I saw myself making decisions with ease regarding Mom's care. I consciously used my ability/power of imagination to visualize all the good that would come from bringing Mom home. I consciously visualized the positive. By doing this I was able to shift myself from fear to faith about Mom coming home.

Paying attention to what I was loving, listening to, and bringing positive music lyrics to mind and finally using my faculty of imagination were some of the ways that I made the most of the principle of mind action. When I found it particularly difficult to focus my thoughts so as to harmonize with the good I know was present, even though there was no seeming evidence, I invested time in prayer/meditation and utilized the spiritual tool of affirmations and denials.

Principle 4: I Pray: Affirmative Prayer and Meditation are foundational spiritual tools I use to remember the Truth of my divine nature.

I had a regular affirmative prayer and meditation practice for two years prior to these events. This was a major change in my life as before I started my practice, I had many issues with prayer. As I became a student of Unity, I learned about the importance Unity puts on the power of prayer and meditation. I was concerned that this emphasis in prayer may be a place in which I could not align with Unity, as the idea of having a prayer and meditation practice was one of the most difficult for me to understand and to incorporate in my own life. I could accept the concept of meditation, but the term prayer was difficult for me. In the past I had even heard positive results about scientific studies of prayer. I did not really believe them since the logic behind them did not fit with my own personal worldview and beliefs.

Many of my issues with prayer arose when my father, Fred, was diagnosed with a terminal illness in 1989 and many people would tell us that they were praying for him. Some of them seemed to think they could perhaps arrange a miracle healing for him due to their own personal connection to "God." I always expressed thanks to these people who offered what seemed to be well intentioned prayers. Inside, however, I resented the fact that they thought they had some special in with "God" and that by beseeching to "him" for a favor, they could help my dad. I thought was this not the same "God" who had afflicted my wonderful father, who as far as I was concerned was as close to walking on water as anyone I had ever known. If this "God" had already done this to my dad I did not see why someone else asking for a reversal of fortune on his behalf would make a difference. I just did not think this was logical. I did not think it worked this way. I found the implication of this notion offensive. Thus, the roots of my resistance to prayer sprouted during this time.

I did not have the same resistance to the term meditation. Meditation just seemed like something that I had no skill or talent for. I viewed meditation as a mysterious process that only the very spiritual were able to participate in. I had a secret envy for those who meditated and did not think I would ever rank among them.

As I started attending Unity and studying the Unity principles I learned about affirmative prayer. Affirmative prayer is just as it sounds: we affirm what we know is true during an investment in a time of prayer (which is reflected in the first 3 principles). There is an official five step prayer process, however, the steps are simply guidelines to help us learn to pray in the affirmative manner. We are to pray in any way that serves us. In affirmative prayer we affirm the Truth and then we sit in Silence so as to know the truth. By affirming the truth, we affirm that Divine Wholeness, Divine Order, and Divine Principle is always at work no matter what is happening in the outer expression of our current circumstances. It is through prayer that we affirm our Christ nature and recognize the Christ nature in each and every other person we interact with.

During our prayer process we invest time in Silence. This is a time of meditation in which we practice silencing our thinking to commune with the One Power, One Presence which is our true divine nature. Investing time in Silence, we recognize the inner divine guidance we need in order to move forward with wisdom in our choices.

Prayer and meditation are a time we dedicate to comprehend and know within the deepest part of ourselves, our true divine nature and to connect to our own inner wisdom (this is sometimes called intuition). Unity recommends a daily practice of prayer and meditation. By the time these events occurred I had overcome my resistance to the concept of prayer and had a regular 10-15 minute practice of affirmative prayer. I have found that by being willing to show up for this practice every day, no matter what, has proven to be highly beneficial. Following through on this commitment was at first challenging since I tended to question whether or not I ever entered "The Silence" and/or if I was affirming correctly. When I took a meditation course at my center, I learned the important thing to remember about having a meditation practice is to just do it. I learned that we should not question the quality of our meditation or whether we are doing it right. When I read this, I thought of Yoda's quote from Star Wars, "Do or Do Not. There is No Try." I added the capitals as I think this is how Yoda would talk! By reminding myself of this from time to time I have stopped judging myself and have been able to follow through on this commitment by "doing" and not "trying."

By practicing affirmative prayer, I was able to move forward with confidence with the idea that we are divine in nature. I knew that all I had to do was listen to the voice inside that would guide me in what to do. I have turned to my practice of prayer and meditation when I was unsure of how to move forward in a relationship. I have turned to my practice of prayer and meditation when I was concerned about someone or worried and I wanted to support them and when I had health challenges of my own. Always after dedicating time to recognizing my own Divine Nature, I felt healthier, stronger and clearer about what to do next. This was true no matter what was happening to me and/or around me. This doesn't mean I didn't and don't still face uncertainty, but it does mean that I know that when I invest time in affirmative prayer and let go of my human need to know (right now) whatever I feel I need to know, that I will move forward with much more confidence and ease in all areas of my life.

When Mom and Sandy were undergoing their health challenges, I turned to prayer and meditation regularly. At home I would sit in prayer and meditation when I had the opportunity to in order to know that although the outer circumstances were negative that in truth, we are eternal perfect Divine Beings. When I found myself unsure about what I was to do next I invested time in prayer and meditation to center myself. By doing this I was able to release some of my negative thinking, worry and stress for instance. By letting go of thoughts that served no functional purpose I had room inside to receive guidance about what was mine to do to help them. I also turned to prayer and meditation when I felt heavy with sadness and pain over what was happening to my family.

Putting prayer in perspective, I turned to it to affirm the truth of our eternal connection, my oneness with Mom and Sandy, and to tune into the guidance I knew was always available. Knowing that through divine law we are all connected, I knew that I could rely on this connection to be where I needed to be and say what was mine to say and do what I needed to do. By affirming this I was able to deny the power the circumstances seemed to have over our ability to thrive.

One of the tools that we use in Unity to shape our experiences no matter what the circumstances are before us, is the use of affirmations and denials. Denials are used to deny the power temporal relative conditions have over us. We do not deny facts. We do not deny our feelings. We do deny that we are powerless over the current circumstances we find ourselves in. We deny that our feelings and negative thoughts have dominion over us. Through denials we gently shift ourselves from fear to faith. We are encouraged to be very gentle with ourselves when we practice denials. We liken the act of denial to as Unity co-founder Myrtle Fillmore said, "gently brushing away a cobweb that is in our way." Denials are an important tool to use in allowing us to let go of negative thoughts. It is by letting go of that which does not serve us that provides room for us to know the Truth.

In these circumstances I didn't deny that Mom and Sandy were suffering physically. I didn't deny the fact of their deteriorating health. I didn't deny that these facts and circumstances made me feel sad, afraid, unsure, guilty, and insecure. I did deny the power these facts and feelings had over me. Through the use of denials, I shifted my focus and attention from the negative view of facts and feeling to a focus on Truth. The Truth being that I had the power/ability of will and I get to choose the experiences I have no matter what the circumstances before me might be.

Making room in consciousness through the use of denials, I was then able to affirm the Truth. By affirming the Truth, I mean recognizing and knowing that Divine Principle is always in place and operating in my life. That in Truth there is One Power, One Presence: omnipotence, omnipresence, and omniscience. Affirming this Truth, I was able to shift my thinking from despair and hopelessness to knowing that divine order is at work even though I cannot recognize it operating at that moment. I was able to remind myself that I AM the place where God shows up. That we are one and our connection never truly began and never ends. By denying the power of the negative seeming facts and difficult feelings had over me and affirming the Truth of my own and everyone I meet's Christ nature, I was charged with zeal and enthusiasm to move forward with doing what was mine to do in order to express my true divine nature. By using the spiritual tool of denials and affirmations I recognized that I had a choice about how I experienced this set of unbelievably difficult circumstances.

I knew that it was important that when we practice the spiritual tools of affirmative prayer, denials, and affirmations, that we carefully avoid the harmful practice called "spiritual bypassing." The term spiritual bypassing was coined by John Welwood, a prominent psychotherapist and author in the transpersonal-psychology field. He defined spiritual bypassing as using "spiritual ideas and practices to sidestep personal, emotional 'unfinished business,' to shore up a shaky sense of self, or to belittle basic needs, feelings, and developmental tasks." (Raab 2019). Our spiritual beliefs, tools and practices were used in order for us to be able to walk these difficult days not in denial of the pain and suffering but in understanding that we were fully equipped to feel what was ours to feel even when it felt like the exact opposite of knowing "good without opposite." I may have said "everything is fine" when it wasn't or been unrealistically optimistic and kept control of my emotions, especially when they were both relying on me for their care. In that sense I may have practiced "spiritual bypassing." Although I think my optimism and hope were not part of that as truly it is in my nature to be hopeful and optimistic. Overall, though, I made a special effort to be present and to avoid being in denial because I recognized the error I made when I pretended things were alright, and I didn't share my feelings when my dad went through the dying process when I was 27 years old. My grieving process for my dad was especially painful, and I believe prolonged because immediately after he died I had so many regrets. I regretted not saying what I needed to say to him and not allowing myself to be fully present to all my feelings as I shared time with him while he underwent the dying process. I had gained the wisdom to be fully present with my own feelings and to Mom and Sandy's feelings during this time. This meant I could be fully present to the beauty and love that was also present as each of us walked through our own personal and collective fires together.

Recognizing that we are timeless beings and witnessing the grace that both Mom and Sandy experienced, I believe that affirming their wholeness was indeed demonstrated. Although neither Sandy nor Mom experienced the miracle of physical healing, I believe we all experienced miracles during this time of challenge. In Unity we define a miracle as an outworking of the natural law that we do not yet understand. It was a miracle to me that I knew that I would be able to get Sandy home to Tucson on Thanksgiving Day safely. It was a miracle that Mom rolled out the crescent rolls. It was a miracle that Mom and Sandy had hospital rooms that were right down the hall from one another. It was a miracle that Joe called when he did, Judy showed up when she did. I was where I was needed almost always. It was a miracle "So Long Farewell" was the song being played on the television when I found out Sandy had died. TK being with me at all was a miracle since we almost lost him a couple of times in the past several years before all this happened. It was a miracle that I could be truly present for both Mom and Sandy as they were undergoing the sacred process of dying.

The greatest miracle of all for me was that I had my spiritual practice to support me during this whole experience. I visited the chapel in both the main hospital and in Peppi's House. I found that spending time in these sacred spaces helped me. I left them feeling comforted and supported. It was a miracle that I knew that although my world seemed to be falling apart, that I knew in truth everything was and always is alright. It was also a miracle that I had found my spiritual family and that they were supporting all of us during this time with their affirmative prayers and support. This meant so much to all of us as well. Everything is a miracle. This is really true.

Principle 5: I Act: I align my actions based on my understanding of these principles.

Moving forward in faith, training and directing my thoughts to what I wanted more of, investing time in Silence and prayer, knowing and affirming our eternal bond and following through on ideas in order to improve our situation, were all actions I engaged in during this this time. The intention behind all that I did was to be a loving supportive presence for the two people I loved most as they were going through incredibly challenging physical and mental difficulties. I was only doing what they would do for me, and they were only accepting my care as I would have accepted it from them. I never took any action with the expectation of getting something back from them in return. In back of all I did was simply the love that I shared with them. In back of all they received was the love they shared with me.

One of the main ways that we were able to live the Truth we know and be loving towards one another, was to find the humor and levity in the situations we found ourselves in. Sometimes the circumstances were so extreme that they seemed absurdly funny. Sandy and I talked several times about how it felt like we were living in a low budget super corny Christmas movie. We found that humorous since we always complained about these movies (we usually watched them with Mom). We agreed that perhaps we had watched more of them than we would have liked to admit. We didn't object to corny movies in general. We just agreed that some of the Christmas movies were particularly ridiculous (like the one where they transport a Christmas tree through a forest fire!). We also found humor in the confusion I caused in the ER the first time I brought them both to the ER on the same day.

Laughter and enjoying the moment were always a part of our family culture. Because of this I tried to consciously do what I could to lighten up the intense situation. I brought gifts into Sandy's room to bring a smile to her face. Every day I tried to think of something that I could bring in to make her smile. I brought in flowers, Star Wars snowflakes, and Best Bud. I also brought in a picture of my dad. This was his high school graduation picture. We had been passing this picture between the three sisters for years as a gag gift. We would always try to sneak it into each other's suitcase, packing boxes, etc. when we were moving or going away. It was a funny picture that Dad never liked of himself. We had fun throughout the years with this picture between Sandy and I and Karen when she was alive. Sandy liked that I brought it into her room. She laughed when she saw it. We also had fun telling others about it when they came into her room.

Sandy and I laughed a lot about my efforts to sleep on the chair in her hospital room. I could never get the back to stay down, no matter how hard I tried. We joked about her looking like a soap opera character when she started receiving oxygen. Patients on soap operas always receive oxygen. That made us laugh about all the silly soap operas and stories we used to follow together. We also laughed about funny song lyrics and silly things like that the night she was in Peppi's House. We had fun joking about the possibility for Peppi's House cruise activities.

Our care givers also added humor and levity to the situation. I will always remember, Leoni, the nurse gave me a good laugh when I told her about Mom's diagnosis and she asked, "Where do you live?" We laughed with the caretakers at Peppi's House over silly things. We laughed about the top secret "spa treatment." Richard, a nurse's aide, got us laughing by telling Sandy to call him Richard Nixon. He joked and called Sandy Miss. Duncan, and he called me Miss. Hayward. I believe he called Mom Miss. Page. He also made Mom laugh when he came in using a towel as if it was a flag for a bullfight. All the attempts at humor were often successful and always deeply appreciated.

We laughed and joked through our tears. It didn't mean we weren't taking the situation seriously. Laughter and levity were a way that we interacted and enjoyed and appreciated life. I treasure all the memories I have of the laughter and shared joy we had throughout these very intense weeks of all our lives.

Another tool we all used was to consciously appreciate these joyful moments and all the good we were experiencing as much as possible. I have learned the value of expressing gratitude when I find myself in difficult appearing situations and find my mind straying to thoughts of despair, hopelessness, sadness, and anger. In the midst of challenging circumstances, I gently remind myself to shift my thinking instead to what I have to be grateful for in that moment. I have found that an attitude of appreciation is the easiest way to move from being a victim to being a victor over what is happening in my life. By making this shift, I remind myself that I do have the power to shape my life no matter what is happening in the outer. I started having a regular gratitude practice seven years prior to these events. Since that time, I have dedicated time each day to list five things that I am grateful for. I am convinced that because of my commitment of seven years to the practice of gratitude that I was able to shift to gratitude relatively easily, even when everything seemed to be going wrong. I also believe that due to my gratitude practice I was able to appreciate all the beautiful moments that happened amidst this seemingly tragic set of circumstances.

I was always appreciative of all the compassion and care given to Mom, Sandy, and myself. I especially appreciated the sacrifice the caregivers made by working on Christmas Eve, Christmas Day, New Year's Eve and New Year's Day. I know it was probably hard for them to be away from their families. I remember asking one nurse about her holiday plans on Christmas Day. She explained that they had celebrated Christmas on Christmas Eve with her 10-year-old son since both her and her husband had to work on Christmas

Day. She said it to me as if it was not a significant inconvenience. I told her how much I appreciated her being there to care for my mother and the other patients. I also asked her to thank her son for his sacrifice and to please let him know what it meant to me to have her taking such marvelous care of my mother on the holiday. I don't know if she told her son this or not. I hope she did.

I was also grateful for all the love that was clearly evident to me as I spent time at the hospital and in hospice. I remember for instance, passing a woman being wheeled on a stretcher on Christmas Day. There was a man walking besides her holding her hand. I did not know them or what their relationship was. All the same I was deeply moved by seeing them together. The love they shared in that moment radiated off them like a beautiful light beacon. I was bathed in the peace and perfection of love at its purest in that moment. I realized at that time that it was not so bad to be at the hospital during the holidays. Where else would I find so much love? Where else do we find the time and mind to put other worldly concerns aside and simply share our love and compassion with one another? I will never forget being a witness to such a beautiful, intimate scene. I will forever be grateful for having that moment when I was reminded that we are all here to love and to be loved in return. Everything else is simply window dressing.

I also appreciated the love, light, and prayers that were sent our way during this time. I was very thankful for the guidance and support that I know we received due to so many holding the high watch for us. It was amazing how many times just as it seemed I was at the end of my rope and was beginning to wonder about what to do that the support we needed showed up. Both support in words, deeds, and prayers. The amazing thing was that this help came with little to no effort on my part to find it.

Here are just a few examples of the fabulous and timely support we received. Our friend and neighbor Justine offered, just in time, to look in on TK when I knew I needed to spend the night with Sandy in the hospital. Terry called to offer to pick up Judy just when I knew I couldn't leave Sandy to go get her myself. Seeing Cindy and being reminded of my wonderful spiritual community at just the right moment. The kind ER doctor gave me a much-needed hug and reassured me that I didn't have anything to feel guilty about when I brought Mom to the hospital that fateful night. Our friend Judy arrived at Peppi's House at just the right moment, knowing how much Sandy wanted her there before she passed on. Sandy's adult foster son Joe, calling Sandy at the perfect time, when Sandy could talk and listen to what he had to say to her. Emails, calls, prayers, meals, flowers, advice, any sign of support and love were met with deep appreciation by us all. I called this time the 7 Card Christmas because we received so many cards: Birthday cards for Mom and me, get well cards for Mom and Sandy, condolence cards for both Sandy and Mom and of course Christmas cards as well! All of these well wishes meant so much to all of us. They were a little bit of much appreciated love coming our way throughout this challenging time.

Mom and Sandy also often expressed their appreciation and gratitude. I remember, for instance, when Sandy saw the oncologist for the last time. Sandy thanked the doctor for her care and how she showed up. Sandy told the doctor about Jill Bolte Taylor's book, *A Stroke of Insight*, and how Jill Bolte Taylor wrote about her experiences as a stroke patient. Jill Bolte Taylor describes in her book how right after her stroke she could sense the energy of the people who came into her hospital room to care for her. She could sense when they came in with the attitude of loving service or when they were there out of a sense of obligation and duty. Sandy thanked the oncologist for coming in with an uplifting, caring and positive attitude. Mom also regularly thanked all the people who cared for her. She was also so thankful for all the cards and letters she received. She had always been the one to initiate sending cards, so I know how much it meant to her to receive them. Both of them also were very thankful and expressed their appreciation to me regularly for the care I gave them. They both had so much cause to complain and yet they both very rarely complained. Instead, they truly saw all the ways in which they were blessed and supported.

I was also very grateful that I was able to support them and be with them during this time. The manager at the Petco store I worked at, Tammy, and the assistant manager, Tamera, were very kind and understanding about the situation. They gave me some time off since I did not see any way I could leave Mom and Sandy alone from that fateful Thanksgiving Day through the holidays. I am eternally thankful for their thoughtfulness and consideration. Knowing I could focus my attention on Mom and Sandy was a huge gift that I never took for granted. It was also with a heart full of love and appreciation for them and my ability to help, that I cared for Mom and Sandy. I never saw anything I did for either of them as an obligation. It was with joy and appreciation for them and for my own capabilities that I cared for them, shopped for them, was there for them, shared in their experience, and loved them during those days when they both were struggling so much physically.

I was also very appreciative of the fact that we did not have to worry about paying the medical bills or the regular bills for either household. Sandy had some concern when she went to the Emergency room the first time, but it was not a big concern. We were blessed to have the resources and insurance coverage to take care of our needs at the time. I recognize how incredibly privileged we were to have the financial means and the ability (access to medical care) to get their medical needs met. I counted my blessing daily in appreciation for the fact that financial support was not among the list of our concerns.

At the end of their physical lives, expressing appreciation and gratitude figured prominently for both Mom and Sandy. Sandy's last words to me were about how much we have to be grateful for. Mom's last words were about how happy she was to be home and how much she loved the Christmas decorations. I think it says a great deal about them both that my last real conversation with both of them was about how grateful they were to be where they were at the time: Sandy in Peppi's House and Mom at home.

My gratitude practice also supported me as I dealt with the fact of losing both of them. When I felt sad about the loss that was to come (and also after they had died), I would remind myself of all the wonderful memories I have of time spent with them. Remembering the gift of years spent together in their loving presence helped me shift from the sadness of loss to the joy of gratitude for all the years we did have together. I also have so much gratitude and appreciation for the wonderful people they both were and the wonderful example they both set for me about how to live a life of purpose and passion.

The practice and art of being grateful truly is one of the most amazing life tools and one I am so grateful that I had at my disposal during this challenging holiday season. I know that due to my years of having a gratitude practice it was much easier for me to see all the beautiful and wonderful ways in which we were supported. Because of consciously exercising an attitude of appreciation we all were able to treasure and value all that we had instead of focusing our attention on the negative facts and circumstances about the situation we found ourselves in. Probably the greatest source of gratitude for each of us was expressed through our love and appreciation for each other. We did get frustrated with the situation, with one another, with ourselves and yet we always quickly forgave what needed to be forgiven and grounded ourselves back in the unconditional love we had for one another.

Sometimes while caring for them, I hurt them by accident. Sometimes I couldn't do all for both of them that I wanted to. Many times, I wanted to be in two places at once. Neither of them ever complained to me about anything I did. When I found myself feeling bad that I couldn't do more I forgave myself. Reminding myself that my intentions were always to do my best to love and care for them, permitted me the ability to forgive myself. When I found Mom on the floor of the bathroom after leaving her alone, I was able to forgive myself for leaving her. When I found myself frustrated by their behavior or choices, I forgave them. We were able to extend this compassion towards one another because behind everything was always the love and eternal connection that we shared. Because we kept kindness and compassion for each other at the forefront of all we did we were able to act with little to no conflict.

Due to my faith in our divine eternal nature and our eternal connection I was able to be honest with myself and with Sandy and Mom when we did receive information about the seriousness of both of their conditions. I knew that as difficult as it was to face the facts of their health challenges, I knew that we are all eternal beings. As eternal beings, the end of our physical life is a time of transition into our next state of being. As such although, I was feeling very sad and fearful about losing my physical bond with Mom and Sandy, I knew with assurance that our connection was never ending. My faith in our eternal bond made it possible for me to talk to the doctors about both Sandy and Mom's condition without being excessively emotional. Because of my faith, I had the strength to be there with both of them as they talked to hospice nurses. This faith was the foundation I stood on as I made phone calls to people who loved them to tell them the news. Making these phone calls was very hard because I knew I was giving people news that would break their hearts and change their lives.

I believe, most importantly, that it was due to my faith that I was able to assure both of them that I was going to be fine on my own. I could say that to them and be sincere. That I could honestly reassure them that I was going to be alright without them was amazing since having them both die so suddenly was such a tremendous loss to me. I was able to let them go. I would regularly remind myself that God stands under everything. God (Sprit) is good without opposite, so I knew we are all always on firm ground whether we know it at the time or not.

Knowing that their eternal souls will carry on beyond the death of their physical bodies kept me in the moment. Being in the moment I was receptive to and appreciative of all the wonderful moments, I had the privilege to share with them during each of their dying processes. Both avowed agnostics, it was interesting to see them both as they became so peaceful, letting go of their current physical bodies and life. Mom became comfortable talking about seeing and embracing those that passed before her when she died. This was not a belief she had held in the past. Sandy wrote beautiful letters for her loved ones to read after she died. She told me that she could never really leave me. What

A JOYFUL SEASON OF SORROW

I experienced as a witness to their courageous brave last days affirmed all I already know to be true. Death is a parting from one stage of living to another.

Our love for one another was the foundation on which we interacted with one another. Because all our intentions were founded on love, I can honestly say I don't have regrets about what I said and did during the time I cared for them. Knowing the truth of our eternal bond, our eternal divine nature, how to use the law of mind action, and to invest time in affirmative prayer and meditation, I was able to take the action needed to shift myself from fear to freedom when I felt my efforts fell short. I am thankful for the opportunity to have been with them as they went through the sacred process that we call death and that I know was truly a time of transition for them from one state of being to a new one.

It truly had been "A Joyful Season of Sorrow." I treasure the memories of this time we shared together. The memories that bring both joy and sorrow. I honor the memory of the emotional and physical challenges that were present as we navigated these uncharted waters together. I honor the strength, courage, wisdom, and love that Sandy and Mom exhibited everyday as they went through the challenges of being mysteriously seriously ill, finding out each of their conditions was terminal and finally going through the dying process. I also honor the memory of the moments of frustration, fear, confusion, and anger that we all experienced because those feelings are part of what makes our strength, courage, wisdom and love all the more powerful and meaningful.

The sorrow of losing their physical presence in my life is something that will always run in the background of my consciousness. That sorrow is only possible because of the joy I had in sharing my life with them. To feel the joy of these memories comes with a measure of sorrow as I no longer have them here to share in these memories and in all the memories of a lifetime of love shared with one another. The memories are all the sweeter in a way now as they are no longer here to create new memories with me.

The memory of the grace of release I felt that embodied and enveloped me in the hospital room as I sat by Mom's bedside on December 18th is something

I regard as one of the most tremendous moments of awareness of wholeness in my life. That moment set the stage for me to be fully present, to be confident in my choices, to allow myself to feel whatever I was feeling without fear, to allow myself to be vulnerable and to ask for help, to know what was mine to do and finally to look back upon this time without regret. During this joyful season of sorrow, I experienced that to be fully human and fully divine is the alchemy where true grace and peace reside.

Wide Open Heart

My heart breaks open.
This is true.
My heart breaks open.
Due to the thought of missing you.
My heart breaks open,
Now and again.
I know this is alright because
I am only human after all.

My heart breaks open.
This is true.
My heart breaks open.
The tears I cry
Come from deep within my soul.

My heart breaks open.
This is true.
My heart breaks open,
Now and again.
I know this is alright,
I am only human after all.

My heart breaks open.
This is true.
My heart breaks open.
The sorrow I feel is real and deep.

My human self doesn't understand
Why you left me.

SUSAN J. SMITH

My heart breaks open.
This is true.
My heart breaks open.
So that it is now bigger than ever.
It's beat stronger and more true,
Then before my loss.

My heart mends with each breath I take.
For I am in Truth
Perfect complete and whole.
I am eternal and so is my bond with all I love.

My heart is now wide open.
This is true.
My heart is now wide open.
So that I can now share my love,
With ever more enthusiasm,
With increased compassion and understanding,
Now at my very core.

Thank you, Spirit,
For my wide-open heart.

By Susan Smith

2012 Gratitude List [this is the letter I sent out with my 2012 Christmas Cards. FYI, Unity of Peace, Tucson is no longer in operation.]

I thought this year I would share the top things I am grateful for in 2012. I have had a gratitude practice for the last 10 years (I list 5 or more things I am grateful for each day). Through this practice I have learned there is always so much to be grateful for.

10. I am grateful that I was able to sell my sister Sandy's house easily to someone I knew would appreciate and enjoy it as much as she did.

I had a wonderful real estate agent, Mike, who went above and beyond to help me. He was even there the whole day I had repair people there. I sold the house to a man named Andy. He was 40 and he was a first-time home buyer. He was in the love with the house and so excited. During our conversations I found out his birthday falls on Christmas day. That seemed so right to me.

9. I am grateful for my good health.

Last year all Mom's and Sandy's doctors kept telling me to get checked out. Well, I did. It was good to have doctors confirm that I am whole and healthy. I am very grateful for the doctors who cared for my family members and for those that are helping me make good health care decisions now.

8. I am grateful to be living in my Mom's wonderful house.

I decided to stay in my Mom's house at least for the foreseeable future. I have very friendly, kind neighbors. I also really like this house. I have made a few changes to make it more my own. I also now have a roommate living with me. That is working out well. I enjoy having the company and it feels right to use the space in the house this way.

7. I am grateful to have the time and resources available in order to settle estate and other business.

I have met many kind and helpful people as I resolved the issues around my mom and Sandy's estate. I have almost everything resolved at this point! I have been taking a sabbatical this year from work. The luxury of having this time to take care of business and to heal has been deeply appreciated.

6. I am grateful for the opportunity to learn and experience new things.

Zumba, trying new healthier recipes and food, my Roku player, connecting my computer to my television, meditation practices, organizing my emails, etc.

5. I am grateful for the wonderful memories I have of time spent with my family.

When I begin to miss my family, I remind myself to be grateful instead that I grew up and had such a warm and wonderful family for so many years. I treasure the memories of the time I spent with each one of my wonderful family members.

4. I am grateful to be an active member of the Tucson Toastmasters community.

Since I have had the time, I love Toastmasters mission and I love my Toastmasters friends I have been very active in service to Toastmasters this past year. I became an Area Governor, have done a Youth Leadership Program at the Boys and Girls Club, helped out with the district 3 Fall Conference, helped out with demonstration meetings and have worked on my own communication and leadership goals.

3. I am grateful to be an active member of Unity Spiritual Center of Peace, Tucson (formerly Unity Church of Peace).

I found this wonderful positive and practical community four years ago. I continue to be very involved with the work of the center and helping with the growth of our expanding community. I became a board member last year. Yes, I am now a member of a church board if you can believe it! I am also involved with the Community Outreach Committee as well as taking courses in order to become a Licensed Unity Teacher. Through my membership with Unity, I have learned spiritual lessons and subsequently developed a spiritual practice that has helped me tremendously.

2. I am grateful for TK the wonder dog!

A JOYFUL SEASON OF SORROW

TK came to live with me full time at the end of last year. He is doing great. I thought when I took him up to Sandy's house, he would look for her, but he didn't. Somehow, he knew that she was no longer with us in the physical world. He turned 15 this December. No one can believe that he could be that old. I did discover he has lost most of his hearing. That hasn't stopped him any. I think if anything, since he can't hear he is bothered less now by outside things. He is a constant source of comfort and inspiration to me.

1. I am grateful for all the wonderful friends and the loving support they have given me during this year of transition.

Beautiful cards and letters, pictures shared, offers to come visit, help with celebration parties, help with garage sale, a compassionate ear, a kind word, a shared meal, going to a movie together, offers to share Thanksgiving/Christmas/Easter, an invitation to a school Celebration for Sandy, a phone call, a chance to serve together… The list goes on. I am so grateful for each person who has helped me during this year of transition. I am so blessed to have been touched by each one of you! Thank you. Happy Holidays everyone!

Love, Sue

EPILOGUE

My heart was broken wide open due to the events described here. Losing the last two members of my immediate family was indeed incredibly difficult. My family had always been the rock on which I set anchor to when life got difficult for me. They were my safety net and my support system. My shelter in the storm. Being the youngest sister, I had thought that I might outlive my sisters, but I never thought that day would come when we all still seemed to have many years of life ahead of us.

I'm so grateful I discovered, developed, cultivated, and practiced the Unity spiritual tools and principles so that when I was left, seemingly alone and on shaky ground, I had a solid foundation of faith, practice, and community to fall back on. I know I would have survived these events without my spiritual foundation, however, I don't think I would have thrived, as well as I have, without my commitment to my spiritual practice, my spiritual understanding, and my spiritual community.

I also think my grieving process was less intense because I applied lessons learned from the past mistakes I made when my father died. This time I made sure I was as fully present as I could be and said what I needed to say to Mom and Sandy before they died. I also think that being grounded in the understanding that we are all timeless eternal beings that cannot in Truth be separated, allowed me to be vulnerable and aware of what was happening and what we were all feeling at the time. Because of these things I do not look back and question the choices I made or the way I behaved. I recognize today that we were all doing the best we could and that is all we can ever expect from ourselves ever.

I was extremely fortunate to have our sweet dog TK with me for most of the next year. He was a constant source of joy and a great companion for me. Having him with me seemed miraculous as he had been diagnosed with cancer himself a couple years before and although we decided not to treat it aggressively (since he was 13 years old at the time). Amazingly, it just disappeared. The veterinarian was really shocked when we brought him in for a checkup six months after his diagnosis. After his miraculous recovery, he went missing for a few days in California along the Colorado River across from Parker, AZ. He somehow was returned to us safe and sound after wandering around (with a cone on his head) in a place he had never been before. The week before Christmas, 2012, he became terribly ill, and we discovered his cancer had returned. It felt like he had been there as my special angel for that year and somehow, he knew that as the year anniversary came to pass that he could move on to his next thing as well. His loving presence was a tremendous gift and something I will always be grateful for.

As the years have gone by, I have experienced the hills and valleys of the grieving process. I've come to understand that the loss of my family will be something that will always be a part of my story. Sometimes I feel the sting of that loss more than others. I honor the feelings of sadness, of loss and of feeling left behind when they come and know that these feelings are a natural extension and come from the privilege of having loved and lost those who loved me unconditionally for my whole life. Within the first year of my grieving process, I remember a weekend of music and connection where I truly felt my heart break open in the best way possible. Faith Rivera, amazing Positive music artist, did a workshop, did the music for our service, and gave a concert at our center that weekend. Her music struck the chord which was holding some of the pain at bay and I felt the cleansing flood of tears of loss, of love, of peace and of release that weekend as I immersed myself in her music.

As time has passed the story of how these events came to pass have lost their prominence as I think of the time I spent with my mom and sister. For a while, some things would trigger my memory of this time of trauma. For a while just seeing a calendar for December 2011 would send a chill down my spine. Now I cherish the memories of laughter, of strength and resilience, of support and love and especially peace and joy that I experienced during that extraordinary time in my life. As time has passed the memories of my family have become wider, deeper and tend to be about our ordinary lives together and not so much about this brief time Sandy, Mom and I spent together.

My life today is rich and full. I am fortunate to have an extraordinary group of friends who support and love me. I've learned how to live without the support of my family members. I've learned how to have minor in-patient surgery without my mom by my side. How to finish a milestone achievement, like becoming an LUT, without my sisters cheering my accomplishment. How to sell the family house without consulting my family for guidance. How to live through a pandemic without my sisters by my side. I miss them most when things happen that I wish they were with me to share, and I know this is just part of my life now as I have the privilege to carry on living.

My spiritual practice, belief system and understanding of principles helps me get through those days when being alone, in a way I never thought I would be, comes to the forefront of my thinking. As I sit in times of meditation and quiet, I gently allow myself to release the feelings of loss and affirm my ongoing connection with those that are as timeless as I am. I call on my mother's commitment to caring for others and amazing ability to learn and grow, my dad's capacity to be kind and to seize the day, on Sandy's passion and commitment to making a positive difference in the world, and for Karen's immense intelligence and talent and deep generosity and compassion to everyone she met. They do live in me and remembering this helps me to be the best me I can be. Mostly I remember the love we shared and know that they are now and will always be cheering me on.

I would not be who I am and could not do what I do without the foundation of love of which I was so fortunate to have been raised with and experienced most of my adult life. My parents taught us by word and by deed to live the Golden Rule. They taught us to follow the example set by Jesus as best we could in how we treat our fellow humans. I am so grateful that I found a faith tradition that teaches the same principle and for all the wonderful practical tools I now have at my disposal in order to keep practicing on doing just that.

I Feel Your Love

I feel your love,
It resides in my heart.
Because of this I know
We can never be apart.

I see your eyes.
They are in my reflection
When I gaze upon myself
In the mirror.

I sense your presence
In the quiet moments
Of my prayer and meditation.

You are with me always.
A presence that I know
Never needs to be questioned.
We are connected.
So, we continue our relationship
Even though we can
No longer exchange hugs, smiles, or a touch.
You are part of my wise council.
Guiding me always in consciousness
To choose what is the best course of action to take
To continue and be
The very best of me.

I feel your love,
It resides in my heart.
Because of this I know
We can never be apart.

By Susan Smith

BIBLIOGRAPHY

Britten, Rhonda. 2001. *Fearless Living. Live Without Excuses and Love Without Regret.* New York: The Berkley Publishing Group.

Carnegie, Dale. 1984. *How to Stop Worrying and Start Living*. New York: Simon and Schuster.

Nahmod, Daniel. 2022. *One Power.* January 17. http://www.danielnahmod.com/one-power.html.

Raab, Diana PhD. 2019. "What Is Spiritual Bypassing?" *Psychology Today.* January 23. Accessed June 16, 2020. https://www.psychologytoday.com/us/blog/the-empowerment-diary/201901/what-is-spiritual-bypassing.

Taylor, Jill Bolte. 2008. *My Stroke of Insight: A Brain Scientist's Personal Journey.* London: Penguin Books.

Unity and New Thought:

There are many Unity and other New Thought Spiritual Centers and Churches that provide both in person and online services that operate on a love offering basis.

- Unity Headquarters: https://www.unity.org/ Source for general information, publications, and prayer requests.
- Unity Worldwide Ministries: https://www.unityworldwideministries.org/. Source for information about Unity Spiritual Centers and Churches.
- Centers for Spiritual Living: https://csl.org/. Centers for Spiritual Living is another New Thought organization (closely aligned to Unity) that also has many Spiritual Centers and Churches.
- International New Thought Alliance: https://www.newthoughtalliance.org/#/.
- Unity Materials Resource Website: TruthUnity.net: https://www.truthunity.net/christianity. There is a tremendous amount of public domain Unity resources available on this website.

Musician websites and information:

- Daniel Nahmod. Website: DanielNahmod.com. Both songs referenced are found on his One Power CD: http://www.danielnahmod.com/one-power.html
- Faith Rivera. Website: https://faithrivera.com/
- Great Resource for Positive Music: emPower Music and Art, Website: https://www.empowerma.com/